Also by David Hughes:

One Act Plays *For Boys*

Five original, one act plays,
written specifically for a small cast of boys.

I0086517

To Rebecca and Francesca.
Because of you, anything is possible.

One Act Plays
For Girls

By David Hughes

VERDICT

No Meat Till Crete

The Perfect Replacement

Have You Seen Down There Lately?

Three Mothers

Beaten Track
www.beatentrackpublishing.com

First published 2012 by Beaten Track Publishing
Copyright © 2012 David Hughes

A CIP catalogue record for this book
is available from the British Library.

ISBN: 978 1 909192 16 4

Cover Photo: adaptation of original by Adam Jones
adamjones.freeservers.com
Cover Design by Beaten Track Publishing

Caution:
All rights in these plays are strictly reserved. Application for public
performances (where a fee may be charged and outside of exam
conditions) should be made before rehearsals commence to:
Beaten Track Publishing, 11 Manor Crescent,
Burscough, Lancashire. L40 7TW.
No performance may be given unless a licence has been obtained.

Beaten Track Publishing,
Burscough, Lancashire.
beatentrackpublishing.com

Contents

Introduction

'One Act Plays For Girls' is my second book in a series aimed at helping teachers and students find texts for exam work.

I believe a performance exam is not like any other assessment. Students want and need to be proud of their work. Therefore, selecting plays that challenge and engage young actors is almost as vital as the final performance itself. Throughout my career I have written plays that were tailored to my students' needs and strengths.

Many of the ideas in my books have come from discussions with students, from something I have seen on TV, or an article I have read in a newspaper. However, the one thing they all have in common is that they are specially designed for young people.

With each play I have detailed the original staging. This is my own interpretation and can be used or discarded at will. This also applies to any stage directions, lighting or sound cues. I have also included short character descriptions, which can be adapted to suit your students' strengths and ability.

All my plays are set in one location, meaning pupils do not have to concern themselves with set changes, giving them more time to focus on their work and to shine on stage.

David Hughes

Verdict

Synopsis

A woman wakes to find herself tied to a chair. A group of mysterious strangers enter and inform the prisoner that she must stand trial for her past crimes. However, both trial and verdict unearth some shocking and potentially life-changing information.

Character Descriptions

Alice – The 'defendant'. She tries to argue her case but is left frightened, scared, alone and fearing the worst. Alice was once strong but is now a defeated woman.

Christina – The leader. She is calm, even under pressure, and leads by example. Her composed nature makes her a somewhat sinister character.

Molly – The loose cannon. Molly is hell-bent on revenge and would rather use gratuitous violence to make Alice pay. She is a disturbed and unhinged character.

Emma – The angry one. Emma is a ball of irate energy and would like to physically punish Alice. She is hotheaded and quick-tempered.

Harriet – The voice of reason. Harriet tries to conduct a fair trial, but is often over-powered by the others. She is a mouse compared with the harsh nature of her peers.

Original Staging

Setting: An unknown area (most probably a disused warehouse of some sort).

Audience: Traverse theatre (two-sided audience).

Set: One chair, four spotlights.

Props: Rope, knives, photographs.

Costume: Everyday wear (Alice); cloaks (the rest of the group).

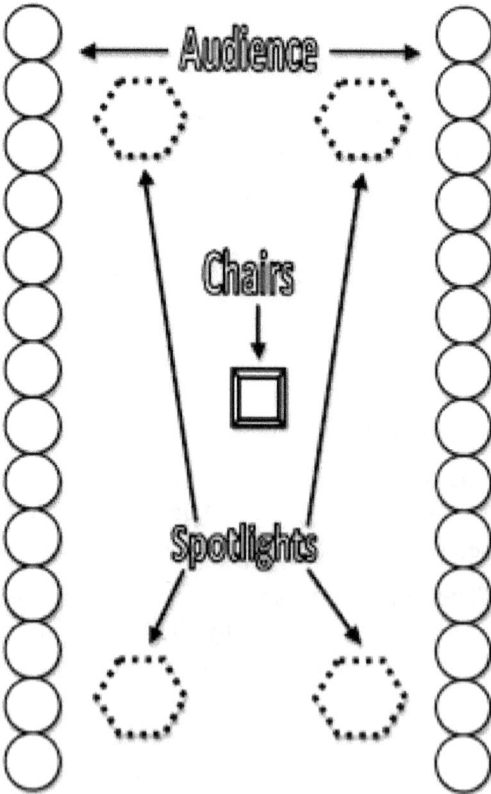

Verdict

A woman (Alice) wakes to find herself sat on a chair. Her hands are tied. Panicking, she tries to remove the rope, but it is proving very difficult to remove. She sits back down in frustration. A voice (voice over) is heard.

Voice: Alice… Alice… open your eyes Alice.

Alice lifts her head.

Alice: *(Scared)* Who's there?

Voice: Alice Gemma Patterson. Do you know why you have been summoned here today?

Alice: *(Scared)* Summoned? I wasn't summoned anywhere! Who are you? And why have you tied my hands?

Voice: I thought that would be obvious. It's so you can't cause any more damage.

Alice: *(Confused)* Damage? Damage to who?

Voice: To yourself. To us?

Alice: *(Scared)* Who are you?

Silence.

Alice: *(Raising her voice)* You can't keep me here. This is kidnap and you can't stop me from leaving.

Alice struggles with the rope, manages to get her hands free and then stands up. As she does, a cloaked figure (Christina) steps in to the light.

Christina: *(Calmly and coldly)* Be carful Alice, your next move could prove vital.

Alice: *(Confused and scared)* Who are you?

Christina: *(Calmly and coldly)* Who am I? What am I? Many questions with many answers. Answers that you will discover… in good time.

Alice: *(Getting braver)* You can't keep me here. You can't just take someone off the streets and force them to stay somewhere. You can't.

Christina: *(Calmly and coldly)* You're right... I can't... but we can.

Three more cloaked figures (Harriet, Molly and Emma) step into the light.

Alice: *(Scared and confused)* I don't understand.

Christina: *(Calmly and coldly)* You will. Please... take a seat.

Alice: *(Defiantly)* I'd rather stand.

Christina: I'd prefer you to sit.

Alice: *(Shouting)* Well I'm not doing what you want!

Emma: *(Angry)* She said sit down... or do you want us to make you?

Long pause. Alice slowly sits down.

Christina: Thank you Alice. Now, where were we? Ah yes, do you know why you have been summoned here?

Silence.

Emma: Answer the question!

Silence.

Christina: Please don't make this situation worse than it has to be.

Silence.

Christina: Fine. But we tried to make it easy.

Christine looks at Molly who moves towards Alice. Molly stands in front of Alice and produces a knife from beneath her cloak.

Alice: *(Panicking)* What are you doing? What the hell is she doing?

Christina: Making you answer the question.

Molly: *(Slow and sinister)* If I'm honest… I'm glad you didn't talk… gives me a reason to start slicing parts of your face off.

Alice: *(Panicking)* Please, please, I don't know why I'm here. Honestly, I don't know why I'm here.

Christina: Is that your answer?

Alice: *(Almost crying)* Yes, yes, that's my answer.

Christina: Good. Now answer the question correctly. Do you know why you have been summoned here?

Alice: *(Shouting with fear)* No I have no idea why I have been summoned here. Is that better? Now can you please tell her to put the knife away?

Molly: *(Snaps in to anger)* Nobody tells me what to do, you bitch.

Molly lunges at Alice with the knife. Alice panics and falls back over the chair. Molly stands over her. Harriet moves to Christina.

Harriet: *(Pleading)* I thought we were just going to scare her?

Christina: Is she not scared?

Harriet: This is too far. *(She turns to Molly)* This is too far.

Molly stops and looks at Harriet. She looks back at Alice and then slowly moves away.

Emma: *(Irate)* What are you doing? Just do it. Finish her off and make her look like the ugly, twisted slut that she is.

Molly says nothing. She simply stands and stares at Emma.

Emma: Fine. If no one has the guts, I will.

Emma moves towards Molly.

Emma: Give it to me.

Silence. Molly looks at the knife and then back at Emma.

Emma: *(Shouting)* Give it to me.

Molly looks at the knife and then at the others. Molly quickly puts the knife to Emma's throat.

Harriet: *(Screaming)* What are you doing?

Molly: *(Sinister)* Nobody tells me what to do.

Emma: You've got five seconds to move it.

Molly: Or what?

Emma: Five…

Harriet: *(Panicking)* Put the knife down…

Emma: Four…

Harriet: *(To Christina)* Tell them to stop this…

Emma: Three…

Harriet: This is not why we're here…

Emma: Two…

Harriet: *(To Christina)* Do something…

Emma: One…

Harriet: *(Shouting)* Molly, don't!

Emma: Zero…

Christina: That's enough.

Silence and stillness. After a long pause Molly removes the knife.

Alice: Molly? Is that your name? Molly?

Molly: *(Calmly but nastily)* We said no names.

Harriet: I'm sorry. I just panicked.

Molly: Forget about it… Harriet.

Harriet: What? Why did you do that? Mine was just an accident.

Molly: *(Sarcastically)* So was mine…my bad.

Emma: *(To Christina)* I told you not to let her do this. I told you she was a nut job.

Christina: You're hardly Mary Poppins now are you… Emma.

Emma looks at Christina in disbelief.

Emma: *(With disbelief)* You bitch.

Molly: Does it really matter if she knows our names? She'll be dead soon anyway.

Alice: *(Scared)* Dead?

Harriet: No that is not happening. *(To Christina)* Tell her that is not happening!

Alice: Please Harriet, help me.

Emma: Oh no! She remembered your name, Harriet. So now you've only really got two options. One… she dies, or two… she lives… and then tells the police who we are and what we've done.

Alice: *(Pleading)* I wouldn't. I won't. I promise. If you let me go I swear I won't say a word.

Emma: *(Spitefully)* Once a liar always a liar. She'll have us locked up before we know what's hit us.

Alice: Not true. I promise; I give you my word.

Alice's statement hugely offends Emma.

Emma: Your word? Your word?

Emma grabs Alice by the face.

Emma: Your word means almost as little as your miserable life.

Alice: *(Crying)* But I don't know what I've done.

Christina: Well maybe now is the time to reveal all… Emma.

Emma pushes Alice's face away and retakes her place in her corner.

Christina: It's time.

The lights change to focus on Alice.

Voice: Alice Gemma Patterson. You have been summoned here to face trial for the heinous crimes committed during your short life. Your answers today will heavily influence the jury's verdict and determine the severity of your punishment. Do you have anything to say before the court is in session?

Alice: *(Defiantly)* Court? This isn't a court. And you're not a jury. And I haven't committed any crimes. And you can't keep me here. So there is no need for me to answer anything because there is no need for verdicts or punishments. This is not happening. So let me go. Now.

The lights flash on the four corners until it stops on Emma. Emma steps forward. She takes her time to circle Alice.

Emma: *(Slowly and deliberately)* So… where should we start?

Silence.

Emma: Come on… you choose.

Alice: I don't know what I'm choosing from.

Emma: So you're admitting there were lots? Interesting.

Alice: *(Frustrated)* I don't know what I'm choosing from because I don't know what you're talking about.

Emma: No? Well let me remind you. *(Pause)* Hinckley and Finch Solicitors. Remember them? I take it by your reaction you do.

Alice: I used to work there.

Emma: You used to work there? Yes… yes you did… didn't you? And when was this?

Alice: Why do you want to know?

Emma: *(Irritated)* You're very arrogant considering the situation you find yourself in. Answer the question.

Pause.

Alice: 2006 to 2008.

Emma: Two years? Such a short time to cause such devastation.

Alice: *(Adamantly)* I was a good worker. I did everything they asked me to.

Emma: And more... so I hear. And why did you leave?

Alice: *(Hesitantly)* Because... I got another job.

Harriet: Objection.

Molly: She's lying.

Christina: Tell the truth please Alice.

Pause.

Emma: *(With a menacing smile)* Let me rephrase the question. Why were you forced to leave?

Alice: You obviously know why.

Emma: For the benefit of the court.

Pause.

Alice: Because... because... I was sleeping with the boss.

Emma: And?

Alice: And... people found out.

Emma: People?

Alice: The others... who I worked with in the office. They found out we were... seeing each other.

Emma: Just the people from the office?

Alice: Yes.

Harriet: Objection.

Molly: She's lying.

Christina: Alice you've been warned… tell the truth.

Pause.

Alice: *(Looking at the ground)* His wife… my boss's wife… she found out.

Emma: His wife? And do you know anything about his wife?

Alice shakes her head. Emma delivers the following speech like a prosecuting lawyer.

Emma: I do. Shall I tell you? Her and her husband, Martin Hinckley, were married for nine years. They had two children, Harry and Sarah, and lived just outside of town in a large semi-detached house with adjoining annex for the in-laws. She and Martin met when they were just fourteen years old. School sweethearts. They married on a beach in Fiji seven years later. They had hoped to travel around Europe together, but plans had to be put on hold when the happy couple discovered they were having a baby. The family was growing. Martin managed to juggle his growing career as a solicitor and impending fatherhood with ease. His wife adored her husband. And he adored her. Fast forward a few years and Sarah, born weighing seven pounds four ounces, completed their family. The four of them were living in bliss. Then one day, Martin mentioned that his company had employed a new secretary. She seemed a hard working girl and he appreciated the extra time she put in after hours. Then things began to change. Arguments between Martin and his wife became a regular thing. Her husband had grown distant; almost like he resented his wife. And then… it happened. A phone call from her husband's business partner. It seems Martin and the new secretary had grown a lot closer than was acceptable. Does any of this sound familiar to you… Alice?

Alice does not answer.

Christina: Answer the question please.

Pause.

Alice: *(Softly)* He told me he was unhappy. He told me they were living separate lives. I loved him.

Emma: *(Angry)* Loved him? You don't know the meaning of the world 'love'.

Harriet: Stick to the facts Emma.

Emma: *(Incensed)* The facts? You want facts? OK, let me tell you the facts Alice. You didn't know Mrs. Hinckley, did you?

Alice: No!

Emma: You never met Mrs. Hinckley, did you?

Alice: No!

Emma: You never even spoken to Mrs. Hinckley, did you?

Alice: No!

Emma: I'd go as far as to say you didn't give a shit about Mrs. Hinckley, did you?

Alice: Why should I? She was nothing to me!

Silence.

Emma: *(Calmly)* She was nothing to you. And yet you made it your business to destroy her life. Thank you. No further questions.

Emma slowly walks back to her corner.

Alice: *(Defiantly)* Is that it? Have you finished your little game? Well let me go then!

The lights flash on the four corners until it stops on Harriet. Harriet steps forward. She does not come too close to Alice and always avoids making eye contact with her.

Alice: What?

Pause.

Harriet: *(Softly)* I need to ask you some questions.

Alice: But I don't need to answer them.

Verdict

Molly: All questions must be answered.

Emma: Guilt will be assumed if you fail to reply.

Christina: Honest responses only please Alice.

Alice stares at Harriet.

Harriet: You went to St Mary's High School… is that correct?

Alice: Yes.

Harriet: What year did you leave?

Alice: *(Defiantly)* I don't remember.

Molly: Try and remember.

Pause.

Alice: Ninety-four… Ninety-five… I don't know.

Harriet: Did you keep in touch with anyone from school?

Alice: *(Obstinately)* You know I didn't.

Harriet: Why not?

Alice: *(Raising her voice)* Because I was a bitch. Is that what you want me to say? I was a nasty, evil little girl who made everyone feel like shit.

Harriet: I want you to tell the truth.

Emma: The truth must be told.

Molly: The truth could set you free.

Christina: The truth will come.

Pause.

Harriet: *(Softly)* Why did you not keep in touch with anyone from school?

Long pause.

Alice: Because I had no friends. Nobody liked me or talked to me. I was the school freak. But I assume you already knew that.

14

Harriet: Nobody liked you?

Alice: Nobody.

Harriet: Nobody tied to talk to you?

Alice: Nobody.

Pause.

Harriet: Nobody?

Silence

Harriet: What about Suzanne?

Pause. Alice slowly realises what she is being asked.

Alice: *(Softer)* Suzanne Haywood? Yeah... yeah she was nice.

Harriet: Was she? So you did have a friend?

Alice: *(Almost smiling to herself)* Yeah. We were the same... Suzanne and me. She understood how hard it was to be... well... to be me.

Harriet: Why?

Alice: I wasn't the only person who was lonely in high school. Suzanne joined in year eight. She was a shy girl, but from the very start I could see she was special.

Long pause. Harriet almost smiles at Alice but manages to control herself.

Harriet: And what happened to Suzanne?

Alice: I don't know. One day we were best friends. And next... she was gone.

Harriet: Gone?

Alice: I came into school one day and the teacher told me she had left and that her parents had moved away. I never heard from her again.

Pause.

Alice: *(Voice breaking)* I loved her.

Harriet almost smiles again. She turns to Christina.

Alice: *(Fighting back the tears)* I don't want to do this.

Molly: We've started.

Emma: Court is in session.

Christina: Go on Harriet. You know this must be done.

Harriet slowly turns back to Alice.

Harriet: You really have no idea why Suzanne left school?

Alice shakes her head. Harriet delivers the following speech like a prosecuting lawyer (albeit much softer than Emma's delivery).

Harriet: Suzanne hated high school. She was bullied and picked on from day one. Her parents moved her schools three times, until she finally joined St Mary's. And then... she met her best friend. Suzanne and Alice were inseparable. They did everything together and went everywhere together. People still called them names, but it didn't matter anymore because they had each other. Then one day, a group of the nasty, popular girls started to pay Alice some attention. They soon became friends and Suzanne got lost... pushed to the back of her best friend's mind. And then... it happened. As Suzanne was changing for a PE lesson, she smelt the rotten odour of stale food and drink. It wasn't until the whole contents of the bin had been dumped on her head that she realised that Alice... her only friend in the world... had made her crash to the lowest point in her life. The laughter was still ringing in Suzanne's ears when she took the razor blade from her dad's bedside cabinet. Her parents found her... covered in blood. Losing her self-respect was one thing... but losing her only friend... that was too much for the young, lonely girl to take.

Long silence.

Harriet: Alice?

Pause.

Alice: *(Devastated)* I don't know what to say.

Harriet: You could start with explaining why.

Alice: *(Ashamed of herself)* Because… I was stupid. I thought those girls wanted to be my friend. They said if I did it they'd… well they said I'd be one of them.

Pause.

Harriet: And did it feel good? To be one of them?

Alice: *(Voice breaking)* I missed Suzanne so much. I still do. I tried to find her. Now I know why I couldn't.

Emma: Suzanne loved you.

Molly: Suzanne was your friend.

Pause.

Christina: And you killed her.

Harriet turns to look at Christina.

Harriet: *(Voice breaking)* I don't want to do this anymore.

Harriet walks back to her corner.

Alice: *(Crying)* I killed her… I killed her… I didn't know… honest… I didn't know.

The lights flash on the four corners until it stops on Molly. Molly steps forward. She moves close to Alice.

Alice: *(Pleading)* Please… just ask your questions… I want to get this over with… please… just get it over with.

Pause. Molly smiles at Alice in sinister manner.

Molly: *(Calm, cold and sinister)* I like your shoes. They look expensive. Do you like expensive things Alice? Do you like to spend money on expensive things?

Alice: Like what?

Molly: Oh I don't know. Like perfume or underwear or holidays… or cars.

Pause.

Molly: What car do you drive Alice? Is it an expensive one? Has it got all the mod-cons? You know: built in Sat Nav, heated seats and all that?

Alice: You keep asking me these questions when it is plainly obvious that you already know the answers.

Molly laughs.

Molly: It's true. I do already know the answers. I'm just trying to figure out if you were telling the truth.

Alice: *(Confused)* About cars?

Molly: About cars. About everything. So go on… answer the question… what car do you drive?

Alice: A Corsa…blue. I've had it for about a year.

Molly: Ever drive anything else? Anything more powerful than *(With venom)* a shitty little Corsa?

Alice: Like what?

Molly: *(Calm, cold and sinister)* Oh I don't know; like a BMW or a Range Rover… or even a Jag.

Silence.

Molly: Have you ever owned a Jaguar Alice?

Silence. Alice looks at the ground.

Alice: My mum had one… a silver one. But I only drove it once.

Molly: *(Calm, cold and sinister)* Oh… are you referring to the little incident back in 1997? Hold on… I think I have some photographs from that somewhere.

Molly moves to Christina and collects some papers..

Emma: For the benefit of the court.

Harriet: Alice will be shown images.

Christina: Some of which are very distressing.

Molly: Here they are. This one is of your car. Not too much damage, is there? Just a scratch down the driver's side and a bit of a bump on the wing.

Alice: I was lucky.

Molly: *(Calm, cold and sinister)* Yes... you were. Not as lucky as the driver of this car though.

Molly shows Alice a second picture.

Molly: For the benefit of the court I am showing Alice the car belonging to a Miss Victoria Lucas. Looks pretty bad... doesn't it?

Silence.

Molly: On the night of the incident you had been drinking... correct?

Alice: *(Cautiously)* I'd had a couple of glasses of wine.

Molly delivers the following speech like a prosecuting lawyer.

Molly: After an argument with your mother, you took her car. You didn't have her permission and you didn't have insurance, but you took it anyway. Upset and annoyed, you drove through the streets like a madwoman, swerving past people and other cars. You narrowly made it through a light before it changed to red and then you turned onto the motorway. You sped up to over nincty miles an hour. It was dark. You were still upset. You'd had a drink. And then... it happened. Victoria Lucas indicated to move in to the second lane, but you weren't in a very charitable mood. You increased your speed and before you could avoid a collision, you clipped the back of Victoria's vehicle. Luckily, you were able to steady your car before driving away. But Victoria... she wasn't so fortunate. By time the paramedics arrived... she was dead.

Silence.

Molly: And yet you escaped without punishment. Please explain to the court how this came to be?

Silence.

Alice: *(Still looking at the ground)* My mum... she told the police that... that the car had been stolen.

Molly: *(Calm, cold and sinister)* Your mum felt she had to lie to the police to save your skin. No one was ever convicted of Victoria's death... until now.

Molly grabs hold of Alice around the throat.

Alice: *(Petrified)* Please, please don't hurt me. I'm sorry, I'm so, so sorry. I'll tell the police everything. If you let me go I swear I'll tell them everything.

Molly goes to hit Alice.

Christina: *(Loudly)* Stop. Let her go.

Molly: *(With hatred)* And who's going to make me?

Christina: *(Calmly)* Molly... we've not finished... this can wait.

Molly looks at Alice before letting go. Molly begins to move back to her corner.

Alice: How did you know... about the accident... how did you know it was me?

Molly laughs.

Molly: That's the best part.

The lights flash on the four corners until it stops on Christina. Christina steps forward.

Alice: *(Confused)* Mum?

Christina: *(Calmly)* Hello Alice.

Alice: Mum what's going on?

Christina: Is it not obvious? You're on trial for crimes against humanity.

Alice: *(Confused)* I don't understand.

Christina: No… you never did, did you? Well if it helps, I am here to explain everything. After all… Mother knows best, doesn't she?

Emma: *(Irritated)* If Mother doesn't hurry up then Mother won't be running the show anymore.

Molly: *(Sinister)* I agree. Get on with it.

Christina: *(Calmly)* All in good time ladies. Now… where were we? Oh yes, I was just about to explain the 'whats' and the 'whys' of this terrible business. I suppose I should start by introducing who we all are. Well, I'm your mother, as you know, and I've known you ever since you were born. These people, however, have known you for considerably less time. This is Emma… I believe you two have already met… but you don't yet know her by her full title. Emma Hinckley. That's right, wife of Martin Hinckley, your lover from your old place of work. And this lady, who you were most recently introduced to, is Molly Lucas… sister of Victoria Lucas… the unfortunate girl who you left for dead at the side of the motorway. And last but not least… this is Harriet... formally known as Suzanne Haywood… your old best friend from high school.

Pause.

Christina: Well say something Alice.

Alice: *(To Harriet)* I thought you were dead.

Christina: No that was just an added extra to the story.

21

Harriet: *(Softly)* My parents changed my name after... well... after I left St Mary's. That's probably why you couldn't find me.

Christina: *(Calmly and coldly)* Well your parents did the right thing Harriet. After all... why would anyone want their daughter to be friends with someone like her?

Alice: *(Confused)* But... I don't understand. How did you... I mean, why are you all here?

Christina: I have to admit Alice that was all my handywork.

Emma: I got a call from you mother offering me the chance to get some revenge.

Molly: Same here. Although I wish we'd have gone with my idea of killing you at the start.

Alice: *(To Harriet)* And you?

Harriet: *(Softly)* I just wanted... I wanted to hear you say sorry.

Silence.

Alice: *(With sincerity)* I am sorry... Suzanne I am so, so sorry.

Christina: *(Calmly)* Too little, too late I'm afraid Alice. Now, if everyone is ready I think it is about time we passed judgement and then proceeded to sentencing.

Alice: *(Voice breaking)* Why Mum? Why do this to me?

Christina: Why? Do you really need me to answer that question? *(With pure hatred)* Because you have brought nothing but shame on me and my family. Because you have caused me nothing but pain and suffering and misery ever since the day you were born. Because you were the biggest mistake of my life. Is that enough of a reason for you Alice?

Pause.

Christina: *(Calmly and coldly)* Now... Alice Gemma Patterson, you have been charged with destroying the lives of anyone you have ever come into contact with. Before the verdict, is there anything you would like to say?

Silence. Alice uses the speech to plead for forgiveness. Throughout the speech Emma, Harriet and Molly exchange glances.

Alice: I know what I've done... and I know I can never change or bring back any of the people who are no longer here. But I am sorry... I am so, so, so sorry. I didn't realise... well, not at the time... I didn't know what I was doing or saying. I am so sorry. And I am not making excuses but... it's all I've ever known. She set the example *(Pointing at Christina)*. She was cruel and spiteful and manipulative. Do you know for my fifth birthday she bought me a bottle of vodka... and when I refused to drink it she forced it down my throat? And when my dad left she beat me so hard that I couldn't walk for a week. And when I got my very first boyfriend she threw herself at him... he was so mortified, he never spoke to me again. I am not excusing my behaviour, in fact, having listened to what you've all said I deserve what's coming to me. But I'm not the only one to blame... because I learnt every bad thing from her... and she knows it. It's why she doesn't want me here anyone... she feels guilty.

Silence.

Christina: A very nice speech but I fear it will not help you now. Time for the verdict. Do you... the jury... find the defendant Alice Gemma Patterson... guilty or not guilty?

Pause.

Harriet: Not guilty.

Christina: *(Enraged)* What the hell are you doing?

Emma: Me too... not guilty.

Christina: *(Getting more angry)* You're forgiving her... for what she's done?

Molly: Full house… not guilty.

Pause.

Christina: *(Mockingly)* You've lost your bottle, all of you. Well I've not.

Christina pulls out a knife and goes towards Alice but the others get in between them first. Molly holds a knife up to Christina's throat.

Molly: *(Incensed)* You lied to the police. You told them the car was stolen.

Christina: I was trying to be a good mother.

Emma: Ha, sounds like you left it a bit late for that.

Christina: *(Trying to convince)* You know what she did… with your husband… you know she nearly killed you… and you know she did kill your sister.

Harriet: *(Adamantly)* No… she didn't do any of that… you did.

Harriet turns to Alice.

Harriet: You need to go… now.

Alice: *(In tears)* But I admit what I've done. I deserve to be punished.

Harriet: You already have… you need to go.

Silence. Alice stands and slowly moves away from the women. She stops and faces them.

Alice: *(With sincerity)* I'm sorry.

Harriet: *(With sincerity)* We forgive you… all of us.

Alice smiles and then leaves.

Christina: *(Angry)* She's getting away. Are you really going to let her just walk out of here without punishment?

Molly: Oh she's been punished enough… you are her mother after all.

Christina: *(Disbelief)* All my planning, ruined. We didn't even get a guilty verdict.

Emma: There's still time for that.

Emma, Harriet and Molly move back to their corners.

Emma: Christina Katherine Patterson… you are changed with crimes against humanity… would the defendant please take her seat in the dock.

The End

No Meat Till Crete

Synopsis

Three Essex girls embark on a holiday with nothing but fun, sun and fit lads on their minds. However, their paradise destination is not quite what they originally imagined and their friendship is tested to its very limit.

Character Descriptions

Chantelle – A ditzy, stereotypical Essex girl.

Justine – A ditzy, stereotypical Essex girl.

Mercedes – A ditzy, stereotypical Essex girl.

Original Staging

Setting: Individual settings (A bus, an office and outside a shopping centre) and then moves on to three sun loungers in a holiday resort.

Audience: End-on theatre (forward facing audience).

Set: Two chairs, three sun loungers.

Props: Mobile phones, shopping bags, (big) handbags, magazines, Saga holiday brochure, make-up, mirrors, objects for bags (tissues, brushes, etc.).

Costume: Stereotypical young female clothing (contemporary), beachwear, towels.

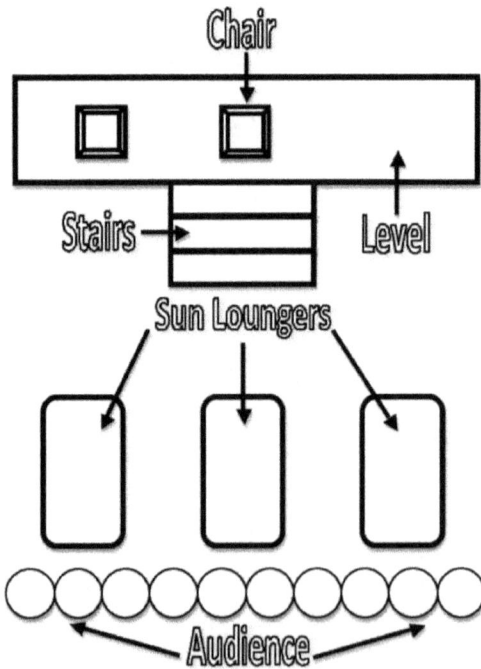

No Meat Till Crete

Lights up. A young woman (Chantelle) is sat at a desk in the middle of the stage. She talks into a headset whilst polishing her nails.

Chantelle: *(Nonchalantly)* Hello Direct Insurance, Chantelle speaking, how may I be of assistance today?... yes... yes... yes... no... no... yes... yes... well you'll need to speak to our customer service team. I'll just put you through *(She presses a button)* Hello Direct Insurance, Chantelle speaking, how may I be of assistance today?... OK and are you the policy holder?... yes... yes... yes... no... no... no... yes... yes... well you'll need to speak to our customer service team. I'll just put you through *(She presses a button)* Hello Direct Insurance, Chantelle speaking, how may I be of assistance today?

A light comes up on a young woman (Justine) who is sat on a bus to the left of the stage. Justine speaks into a mobile phone and is clearly annoyed.

Justine: Chantelle, it's Justine.

Chantelle: Oh hiya babe. Where are you?

Justine: Oh I don't even wanna talk about it.

Chantelle: What's wrong babe?

Justine: I'm on... a bus.

Chantelle: On a bus?

Justine: On a bus.

Chantelle: What you doing on a bus?

Justine: Had to, didn't I? Bleedin' Dad wouldn't give me a lift.

Chantelle: *(Exaggerated)* No!

Justine: Yeah. Said he was fed up of being my personal taxi service.

Chantelle: *(Even more exaggerated)* He never!

Justine: He did.

Chantelle: Did he?

Justine: He did.

Chantelle: I haven't been on a bus in years.

Justine: *(Disgusted)* You don't want to Chantelle. It stinks.

Chantelle: Does it?

Justine: It does.

Chantelle: What of?

Justine: It's like a sort of… wee smell.

Chantelle: *(Shocked)* Shut up!

Justine: It's disgusting.

Chantelle: Who wees on a bus?

Justine: I know.

Chantelle: It's disgusting.

A phone rings. Chantelle rummages in her handbag.

Chantelle: *(To Justine)* One second babe *(Chantelle answers the mobile phone)* Hello.

Lights up on the right of the stage. A young woman (Mercedes) is stood holding shopping bags. She talks into her mobile phone.

Mercedes: Chantelle, it's Mercedes.

Chantelle: *(To Mercedes)* Oh hiya babe. *(To Justine)* It's Mercedes.

Justine: Oh hiya babe.

Chantelle: *(To Mercedes)* Justine says hiya babe.

Mercedes: Oh tell her I said hiya babe.

Chantelle: *(To Justine)* Mercedes says hiya babe.

Mercedes: Aw… where is she?

Chantelle: *(To Mercedes)* She's on a bus.

Mercedes: A bus?

Justine: Tell her it stinks of wee.

Chantelle: *(To Mercedes)* And it stinks of wee.

Mercedes: *(Confused)* She's on a bus that stinks of wee?

Chantelle: *(To Mercedes)* It's well bad.

Justine: Well bad.

Mercedes: *(Confused)* What's she doing on a bus that stinks of wee?

Chantelle: *(To Mercedes)* Her dad made her.

Mercedes: Shut up, he didn't!

Chantelle: *(To Mercedes)* He did.

Justine: Said he wouldn't be my personal taxi service.

Chantelle: *(To Mercedes)* Said he wouldn't be her personal taxi service.

Mercedes: That's well awful.

Chantelle: *(To Mercedes)* Really well awful.

Justine: Well bad awful.

Mercedes: Well it's a good job I called then coz I've got some news.

Chantelle: *(To Mercedes)* Shut up! What news?

Justine: What's the news?

Chantelle: *(To Justine)* Merci's got some news!

Justine: What is it?

Chantelle: *(To Justine)* Don't know. She just said she's got some news and it's a good job she called.

Mercedes: You're gonna love it.

Justine: *(Excited)* Oh I'm so excited. I love news.

Chantelle: *(To Justine)* Me too.

Mercedes: You ready for this?

Chantelle: *(To Mercedes)* Go on.

Justine: I wanna know.

Chantelle: *(To Justine)* I'll tell you in a second.

Mercedes: Tell me what? Have you got news too?

Chantelle: *(Mercedes)* No, I've not got any news.

Justine: You haven't got any news? Then why did she say she had news?

Chantelle: *(To Justine)* No, Merci's got news but I haven't got news.

Mercedes: I'm confused.

Justine: I'm confused.

Chantelle: We're all confused.

Short pause.

Mercedes: I've got it!

Mercedes rummages through her handbag and pulls out another mobile phone. She dials a number and after a few seconds a phone is heard. Justine rummages through her handbag and pulls out a second mobile phone. She answers.

Justine: Hello.

Mercedes: *(To Justine)* Oh hiya babe, it's Mercedes.

Justine: *(To Mercedes)* Oh hiya babe. *(To Chantelle)* It's Mercedes.

Chantelle: I was just talking to her!

Mercedes: You still are.

Justine: This is genius! You're so clever Merci!

Mercedes: Aw thanks darlin'!

Chantelle: *(Confused)* How is this happening?

Mercedes: Forget about that. I've got news. Do you remember I said that my mum was going on her holidays?

Justine: Yeah. Corfu wasn't it?

Chantelle: No it was the Costa wasn't it?

Mercedes: It's Crete. Anyway… she's only gone and broke her leg.

Silence.

Justine: *(Sympathetically)* That's terrible news.

Chantelle: *(Sympathetically)* Terrible. What happened?

Mercedes: *(Uncaring)* Don't know. Something about too much Sambuca and her BMW. Anyways, it means she can't go on her holidays.

Justine: *(Sympathetically)* That is terrible news.

Chantelle: *(Sympathetically)* Your poor mum.

Justine: She must be dev-oed.

Chantelle: Well dev-oed.

Mercedes: *(Still uncaring)* She'll get over it. Anyways, because of some clause in her insurance contract she's not able to claim the money back and my Aunt Mary and Aunt Kathy says they don't wanna go without my mum so none of them is going.

Justine does an intake of breath.

Justine: This story just gets sadder and sadder.

Chantelle: Your poor mum and poor Aunt Mary and poor Aunt Kathy.

Mercedes: *(Still uncaring)* They'll get over it too.

Short pause.

Justine: Can I say something Merci? And don't get me wrong coz I knows you love your mum and that. But you don't seem... well... you don't seem very sad about your mum and her leg and the holiday and your Aunt Mary and Aunt Kathy and things.

Short pause.

Mercedes: And why do you think that is?

Pause.

Chantelle: *(Shocked)* No!

Mercedes: *(Excited)* Yes!

Justine: *(Confused)* What?

Mercedes: *(Excited)* Yes!

Chantelle: *(Shocked)* No!

Mercedes: *(Excited)* Yes!

Justine: *(Confused)* What?

Chantelle: *(Shocked)* No!

Mercedes: *(Excited)* Yes!

Justine: *(Confused)* What?

Chantelle: Really?

Mercedes: *(Excited)* Really?

Justine: *(Confused)* What?

Mercedes: *(Excited)* One week!

Chantelle: All week?

Justine: *(Confused)* What week?

Mercedes: *(Excited)* All inclusive!

Chantelle: All inclusive?

Justine: What's inclusive?

Mercedes: *(Excited)* Sun!

Chantelle: Sun!

Justine: *(Confused)* Sun?

Mercedes: *(Excited)* And fun!

Chantelle: Fun and sun!

Justine: *(Confused)* Fun sun?

Mercedes: *(Excited)* It will be well reem!

Chantelle: Proper reem!

Mercedes: *(Excited)* The reemist!

Chantelle: Reem on top of reem!

Justine shouts to be heard.

Justine: Can someone just tell me what this all inclusive sun fun reem thing is?

Silence.

Mercedes: Tell her Chantelle.

Silence.

Justine: Well?

Silence.

Chantelle: I don't know what she's on about.

Mercedes: For God's sake! My mum and my two aunties can no longer go on their holiday. That means that there are three spare tickets to an all-inclusive holiday to Crete. Three. Not one, not two, three. So my mum needs to find three people who like lying in the sun, sipping cocktails, whilst being surrounded by gorgeous blokes.

Silence.

Justine: *(Sincerely)* Oh I hope she can find someone soon.

Chantelle: *(Sincerely)* Yeah. It's a shame we didn't know about this earlier. Us three would have had a well good time.

Pause. Chantelle sudden realises.

Chantelle: Hold on…

Pause.

Chantelle: *(Shocked)* No!

Mercedes: Yes!

Chantelle: *(Shocked)* No!

Mercedes: Yes!

Justine: *(Confused)* What?

Chantelle: *(Shocked)* No!

Mercedes: Yes!

Justine finally realises.

Justine: *(Shocked)* No!

Chantelle: *(Shocked)* No!

Mercedes: Yes!

Justine: *(Excited)* Yes!

Chantelle: *(Excited)* Yes!

Mercedes: *(Excited)* Yes!

All three girls scream with delight.

Mercedes: Can I just check? You do know that it's us three that are going?

Justine: *(Excited)* Yes!

Chantelle: *(Excited)* Yes!

All three girls scream with delight.

The three girls change into their holiday clothes. They each grab a large bag and meet (centre stage). A sound of a plane landing is heard. The three girls step forward to the top of the stairs.

Justine: Watch out Crete coz here we come…

The sound of wind is heard. They stare at each other with confused looks. They struggle down the stairs with their cases. At the bottom there are three sun loungers.

Justine: It's a bit… well… dead, innit?

Mercedes: A bit… yeah.

Justine: Maybe no one is awake yet?

Chantelle: It's three in the afternoon.

Mercedes: Maybe everyone was out partying till like seven in the morning so they're all still asleep.

Justine: Yeah! Yeah that sounds like it. Do you think Chantelle?

Chantelle: Defo Justine. Let's top up the tan before all the fit lads show up.

Mercedes: Totes.

Justine: Tote totes.

The three girls sit on their sun loungers. They prepare themselves for sunbathing. After a short while they realise it is a bit too cold.

Justine: It's a bit cold innit?

Mercedes: Yeah, it is a bit innit?

Chantelle: Yeah it is a bit.

Pause. The girls pull out something warm to put on.

Mercedes: *(Excited)* I can't wait for these fit lads to show up.

Justine: *(Excited)* Me too.

Chantelle: There are no fit boys back home.

Justine: None at all.

Mercedes: All proper mingers.

Pause.

Chantelle: Except Billy.

Justine: Oh Billy's well fit.

Mercedes: Totes fit.

Pause.

The three girls pull out something else warm to put on.

Chantelle: Just a matter of time girls.

Justine: Any minute now.

Mercedes: *(Excited)* I literally cannot wait.

Pause. Justine sees someone across the pool.

Justine: Hold on... here's one now.

Chantelle: Right quick look busy.

The girls grab magazines from their big bags and pretend to read. They peer over the top at their eye candy.

Mercedes: *(Almost whispering)* Well... what does he look like?

Chantelle: *(Almost whispering)* I can't see. He's stood with his back to us.

Justine: *(Almost whispering)* He's tall.

Mercedes: *(Almost whispering)* How tall?

Justine: *(Almost whispering)* About the same as Frankie.

Chantelle: No, he's much taller than Frankie.

Mercedes: Which Frankie are we talking about?

Justine: Frankie from the tanning shop.

Chantelle: Oh, I was on about Frankie from the bar.

Mercedes: Well is he as tall as Frankie from the tanning shop or Frankie from the bar?

Chantelle: *(Panicky)* Oh wait, he's coming over.

Justine: *(Excited)* This is it. I'm so excited.

Mercedes: Just play it cool girls, play it cool.

The girls pretend to read their magazines. An elderly voice (voiceover) is heard.

Voice: Excuse me ladies. Do you know what time the aqua aerobics start?

The girls slowly look up from their magazines. Their faces are a mixture of shock and disgust.

Voice: I said do you know what time the aqua aerobics starts?

The girls shake their heads.

Voice: No bother. Thank you anyway ladies.

The girls watch as the voice walks away.

Justine: *(Disgusted)* What the hell was that?

Mercedes: *(Disgusted)* He must have been about a hundred.

Chantelle: *(Nearly in tears)* I'm pretty sure I could see something popping out of his thong.

Justine: That is so disgusting.

Mercedes: I actually feel physically sick.

Chantelle: Me too.

Pause.

Justine: Do you know what?

Chantelle: What?

Mercedes: What?

Justine: I don't think I've seen anyone else since we got to this hotel.

Mercedes: Me neither.

Chantelle: Course we have. What about the guy on reception?

Mercedes: You mean the old guy?

Chantelle: And the woman who showed us to our room?

Justine: You mean the old woman?

Mercedes: Has anyone seen any actual hotel guests?

The girls pause to think.

Justine: Well there was aqua aerobics man with the green thong.

Chantelle looks across the pool.

Chantelle: And I can see an old couple sat on the other side of the pool.

Mercedes: And there were those two old ladies who got into the lift after us.

Silence. Chantelle looks at Mercedes.

Chantelle: *(Suspiciously)* Mercedes?

Mercedes: Yeah.

Chantelle: Who did your mum book this holiday with?

Mercedes: My Aunt Mary and Aunt Kathy.

Justine: Aww I love your Aunt Mary and Aunt Kathy.

Chantelle: No. I mean, which holiday company did she book it with?

Mercedes: Oh... I don't know. Hold on... I think she gave me the holiday brochure before we left.

Mercedes searches through her bag. She pulls out lots of other things before she gets to the brochure.

Mercedes: Here it is.

She passes the brochure to Chantelle. Chantelle looks at it for a few seconds. Her faces changes to reflect her shock.

Chantelle: I don't believe this.

Justine: What?

Mercedes: What don't you believe?

Chantelle: Mercedes... how old is your mum?

Mercedes: No idea. Why?

Chantelle: Coz she's booked this holiday with a company called Saggy.

Chantelle holds up a 'Saga' brochure. Justine snatches the brochure.

Justine: *(Disbelief)* You've got to be kidding me.

Mercedes: You're telling me this is an old people's holiday?

Chantelle: Well we haven't seen anyone under the age of seventy have we?!

Mercedes: I don't believe this.

Short pause.

Justine: Girls... it gets worse.

Mercedes: Worse?

Chantelle: How can it get any worse?

Justine: *(Reading from the brochure)* It says this hotel is ideal for the over fifties and situated in isolated bliss away from the hustle and bustle of the island's nightlife.

Silence.

Mercedes: *(Almost crying)* You mean... no clubs?

Justine: No clubs.

Chantelle: What about bars and restaurants?

Justine: No bars... no restaurants.

Mercedes: *(Almost crying)* Justine... please tell me we're near a beach.

Justine looks in the brochure. She eventually looks up with a look of terror on her face.

Mercedes: *(Dramatically)* I think I'm gonna pass out.

Chantelle tries to stay positive.

Chantelle: It's not as bad as we think. If we've ended up here then some fit lads might end up here too.

Justine: Chantelle's right. We just need to stay positive.

Mercedes is taking deep breaths.

Mercedes: *(Dramatically)* I can't feel my legs.

Chantelle: Right, let's just pretend we don't know where we are and I'm sure things will work out just amazeballs.

Justine: Yeah. Just act causal.

The girls try to act casual. After a few seconds Justine stands up.

Justine: *(Defiantly)* I can't do it.

Chantelle: Do what?

Justine: Pretend that this is gonna be fun when it's clearly not.

Mercedes: *(Almost crying)* I'm so sorry Justine. I didn't know, honest.

Justine: *(Getting angry)* Well you should have bleedin' checked.

Chantelle: Hang on Justine, this isn't her fault.

Justine: Well whose is it then?

Mercedes: She's right Chantelle. It's all my fault.

Chantelle: You didn't mean to bring us on an old people's holiday.

Justine: But she did, didn't she?

Mercedes: *(Almost crying)* I did Chantelle.

Chantelle: Yeah, but you didn't know it was an old people's holiday did you?

Silence.

Chantelle: Did you Mercedes?

Silence.

Chantelle: *(Angry)* Mercedes? Did you know this was an old people's holiday?

Mercedes: No. But my mum did go on about us being respectful to the other guests coz of their age and everything.

Justine: This is not happening!

Mercedes: I just thought she meant the Greeks were mature.

Chantelle is still trying to be positive.

Chantelle: Well we're here now so we might as well make the most of it.

Justine gets her mobile phone out.

Chantelle: What are you doing?

Justine: Calling my dad. I'm getting the first flight out of here.

Chantelle: You are so over-reacting.

Justine: Did I ask for your opinion Chantelle?

Mercedes: *(Almost crying)* This is all my fault.

Chantelle: You're upsetting Mercedes.

Justine: *(Defiantly)* Good. This is all her fault. Why isn't my phone working?

Mercedes: You need to set it up to work abroad.

Justine: Did I ask you?

Chantelle: Just ignore her Mercedes. We'll have a good time without her.

Justine: This is so typical. Looks like I'm stuck in this bleeding place.

Chantelle: Well don't expect us to talk to you with an attitude like that.

Justine: Fine.

Chantelle: Fine.

The three girls sit in silence on their sun loungers. The tension is evident.

Mercedes: Chantelle?

Chantelle: Yes babe?

Mercedes: I want to go home.

Chantelle: Everything's going to be good babe. We just need to let things settle.

Silence.

Mercedes: Chantelle?

Chantelle: Yes babe?

Mercedes: I really want to go home.

Chantelle: Merci… I've already said… we need to let things sink in and we'll feel better. Trust me.

Silence.

Mercedes: Chantelle?

Chantelle: *(Raising her voice)* For God's sake Mercedes! What do you want me to do? Do you want me to just magic up a plane to pick us or something?

Mercedes: I just want…

Chantelle: I didn't cause this mess but I am trying to make the most of a bad situation. So can we please just stop talking about going home and have a good time!

Short pause.

Chantelle: I can't. You've ruined it for me now. Both of you. Ruined it for me.

Chantelle starts to pack her things away.

Justine: What is she doing?

Mercedes: I think she's gone mad!

Chantelle: *(Almost crying)* I tried to make it work but too much has happened so that's it. I'm going. I don't know where I'm going but I am going. Gone. I am going and nothing is gonna stop me. It's ruined and I am going.

Justine see's something across the pool.

Justine: *(Shocked)* I don't believe this.

Chantelle: Well believe it coz I am not changing my mind.

Justine: No… look.

Mercedes: *(Shock)* O.M.G. Chantelle, you were right.

Chantelle: Well it's a shame you didn't realise that earlier coz it's too late girls. I am going.

Pause.

Chantelle: What do you mean I was right?

Justine: Look.

Chantelle looks across the pool.

Mercedes: *(Excited)* How many are there?

Justine: I can see three.

Mercedes: And are they… fit?

Justine: *(Excited)* Yes… totes fit.

Chantelle: *(Panicking)* They're coming over. Oh my God they're coming over. Quick, act casual.

The girls grab their magazines and pretend to read. A voice is heard (voice over).

Voice: Excuse me girls.

The girls pretend not to hear.

Voice: Er… I was just wondering if… er… if my mates and me could join you?

The girls casually look up.

Chantelle: *(Casually)* I suppose so. If you don't mind, girls?

Justine: *(Casually)* I don't mind Chantelle.

Mercedes: *(Casually)* I don't mind either Chantelle.

Chantelle: *(Casually)* No we don't mind.

Voice: Cool. I'll just tell the lads.

The girls watch the voice move away. As soon as he is gone they quickly search in their bags and grab make-up and apply as fast as they can. They bring out huge mirrors with everything attached (tampons, tissues, bits of underwear, etc). As soon as they've applied they try to act casual. They just have enough time to give each other a little smile.

Voice: Hi girls. This is Tom and Paul. And I'm Ollie. Where should I sit?

All three girls: Here.

They all point next to each other. They quickly look at each other and scowl.

The End

The Perfect Replacement

Synopsis

Four friends meet for one of their regular dinner parties. All is well until a new lady, invited by the host Stephanie, arrives, sending shock waves throughout the group. The reason? Their new guest forces them to remember a time they would much rather forget.

Character Descriptions

Stephanie – The host of the party. She is sociable, confident and creates a positive atmosphere. However, as the story develops she turns into a woman focused on revenge – and in the most humiliating way.

Maria – A sweet-natured woman whose kindness and gentle manner makes her popular within the group. As the story develops she becomes a nervous wreck and appears close to a breakdown.

Sophia – A woman with a quick temper. Sophia is a happy person but can often appear irritable and 'snappy'. She is honest and trustworthy and will not be taken for a 'mug'.

Abigail – Honest to a fault. Abigail can seem harsh but has earned the respect of others through her frankness. She is direct and clear.

Wendy/Jennifer – Wendy is the new member of the group. She is shy but wants to fit in. Jennifer causes friction during the party. When confronted she fights and appears callous and cold.

Original Staging

Setting: A house (dinner table).

Audience: End-on theatre (forward facing audience).

Set: Five chairs, dinner table, entrance door, exit door to kitchen.

Props: Dinner tableware, wine bottles, present box, card, flower, shampoo bottle, hand towel, receipt.

Costume: Posh dinner party dresses (think 'Desperate Housewives').

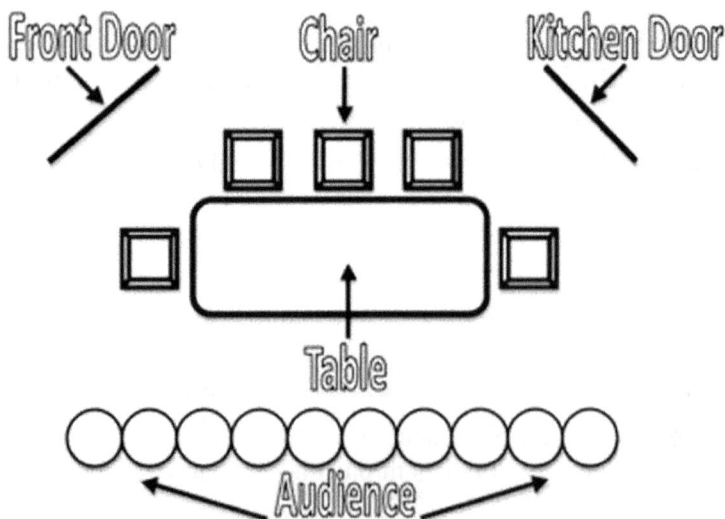

The Perfect Replacement

A dinner party. Stephanie is busy arranging the table. She seems very pleased with herself. The doorbell rings. Stephanie disappears off stage. She re-enters a few seconds later followed by Sophia and Maria. They are both smartly dressed and carrying bottles of wine.

Maria: You shouldn't have gone to so much trouble, really you shouldn't.

Stephanie: *(Playfully dismissive)* Oh it's no bother. Kevin is away for the weekend and you know how I like to keep busy.

Maria: Well it's just lovely. I particularly like the cut of this tablecloth. You must give me the number of your seamstress.

Stephanie: No seamstress Maria, just a bit of patience and Issac Singer's best machine.

Maria: Well I am impressed. Did you hear that Sophia? Stephanie made the tablecloth herself.

Sophia: (*Unenthusiastically*) Yes... fascinating.

Maria: *(To Stephanie)* Well you must give me a lesson soon. I'm not sure my hands are quite as delicate as yours, but I would love to learn the ways of the needle.

Stephanie: It's a deal.

The doorbell rings.

Stephanie: Please excuse me ladies.

Stephanie exits.

Sophia: *(Patronizingly)* You don't have to suck up to her all the time you know.

Maria: *(Offended)* I am not sucking up to anyone. I'm simply showing our host some common courtesy.

Sophia: Well do remember dear... it's only a tablecloth.

Stephanie enters followed by Abigail.

Stephanie: Look who I found ladies.

Maria: *(Excited)* Abigail darling. That dress is stunning. And have you lost weight?

Abigail: I have. And you are very kind for noticing. *(A cold greeting)* Sophia.

Sophia: *(A cold greeting)* Abigail.

Abigail: Well… what do you think? Does the dress look nice?

Sophia picks her words carefully but deliberately.

Sophia: It's very… clingy.

Maria tries to save the situation.

Maria: I think she means shapely.

But Sophia stands by her statement.

Sophia: No, I mean clingy.

Abigail: *(Proudly)* This was a little present from Robert. He was ever so pleased with me about the weight loss. Took me straight to Harrods and told me to choose anything I liked. Well… within reason.

All laugh, except Sophia.

Maria: Well it looks lovely Abigail. Doesn't it Stephanie?

Stephanie: Very stylish.

Abigail: *(Showing off)* Well so it should. Those last few pounds were a bugger to shift.

Maria: How much have you lost in total now?

Abigail: Guess?

Awkward silence.

Abigail: Go on guess. I won't be offended if you're wrong.

Awkward silence.

Abigail: Come on Maria, how much?

Maria: *(Hesitantly)* Er… well… I'd say it has to be in the region of… a stone?

Abigail stares at Maria.

Maria: And a half?

Abigail continues to stare at Maria.

Maria: Plus another half?

Abigail: *(Proudly)* Very nearly. Two stones, three pounds.

Sophia nearly chokes on her wine.

Abigail: Something the matter Sophia?

Sophia: No, no, nothings wrong.

Sophia speaks just to Stephanie.

Sophia: Two stones? Not with arms that size.

Stephanie ignores the comment and speaks to the others.

Stephanie: Now ladies, as we're all here I've got a little announcement to make.

Abigail: Oh let me grab a glass for the toast.

Stephanie: No, it's nothing like that. Well… as you all know, it's been over six months since… well, it's been a while since we last had one of our little get togethers and I thought it might feel a bit… empty with just the four of us. So I've invited someone else.

The other women look shocked.

Maria: You've invited a fifth person?

Stephanie: I have.

Abigail: And do we know her?

Stephanie: *(Causally)* I doubt it. She's new to the area. Moved in across the road last Tuesday.

Maria: Tuesday?

Abigail: Who moves house on a Tuesday?

Stephanie: *(Causally)* Her husband is away on business for long periods of time and I thought she could use the company.

The others are stunned in to silence.

Stephanie: I'd appreciate your thoughts ladies.

Silence.

Sophia: *(Cautiously)* Don't you think it's a bit… soon?

Stephanie: Well how soon is too soon Sophia?

Maria: She does have a point Stephanie. Six months may have passed but I can still… *(Her voices breaks a little)* well… I can still remember.

Stephanie: *(Reassuringly)* We all remember darling, but that doesn't mean we shouldn't move on.

Sophia: There's moving on and there's moving on too fast. (*Pause*) Listen, I'm not too sure I feel comfortable about this. I might give Michael a call and ask him to collect me.

Sophia gets up to leave.

Stephanie: Oh Sophia, please don't leave. Wendy really is a lovely lady.

Maria: Wendy?

Stephanie: Wendy Hilton. Married. Two beautiful children. She really is the perfect replacement.

Pause.

Abigail: *(Avoiding eye contact with Stephanie)* I didn't even know we were in the market for a replacement.

Stephanie: *(Directly)* Life goes on Abigail.

Abigail: Evidently it does.

Sophia: Well life is moving on a little too fast for me. I'll say goodnight ladies.

Sophia exits.

Abigail: *(Sarcastically)* Well this has been delightful.

Abigail finishes her drink and the gets up to leave.

Maria: *(Pleading)* Can't you just stay for a while darling? Stephanie really has gone to a lot of trouble. She's even made her own tablecloth.

Abigail: No it's best I go. The night has been soured and I'm not sure the positive atmosphere I brought into the room can be salvaged. Goodnight ladies.

Abigail turns to leave. She stops. Sophia is stood in front her.

Abigail: I thought you'd gone?

Sophia looks and sounds petrified.

Sophia: I did... well, I had... but I met someone... at Stephanie's front door... (*To Stephanie*) Is this some kind of joke?

Stephanie: *(Confused)* I beg your pardon?

Sophia: Have any of you ever met this Wendy woman?

Maria: No.

Abigail: You know we haven't. Can someone please explain what is going on here?

Stephanie: I'm afraid I have no idea what she is talking about.

Sophia: *(Getting angry)* This is either a huge coincidence or cruel joke at our expense. Which is it?

The all look at Stephanie.

Stephanie: I really don't have a clue what Sophia means.

Silence.

Sophia: OK. Your guest is waiting at the door.

Stephanie looks at the others before exiting.

Maria: What was all that about?

Abigail: *(Provokingly)* You really have made this evening feel very awkward Sophia.

Maria: What was all the huge coincidence or cruel joke thing about?

Sophia: I need a drink.

Sophia starts to pour herself a drink. She is shaking so much that she spills a bit of wine.

Maria: You really are not making any sense darling.

Abigail: Nothing new there if you ask me.

Sophia: *(Raising her voice)* Don't push it tonight Abigail, I mean it.

Abigail: Oh somebody is in a bit of grump aren't they? What a night we're in for!

Maria: Abigail, please, tell me what the matter is. Oh my word, you're shaking. Why are you shaking?

Sophia finishes another drink.

Sophia: You're about to find out why.

Stephanie enters followed by Wendy.

Stephanie: The others are really looking forward to meeting you. Ladies… this is Wendy Hilton.

Maria, Sophia and Abigail stare at Wendy in silence.

Wendy: *(Nervously)* Hello. Thank you for inviting me tonight… it's a pleasure to meet you all.

Silence.

Stephanie: Wendy has brought a bottle of red, isn't that nice? I'll just open it and let it breathe. Ladies, why don't you make Wendy feel at home?

Stephanie leaves. Maria, Sophia and Abigail stare in silence and do not move.

There is a long awkward silence. Wendy tries to make conversation.

Wendy: This is a lovely house. Has Stephanie lived here long?

Silence.

Wendy: I've just moved in across the street. Number thirty-two.

Silence.

Wendy: Needs a bit of redecoration but generally the place is very nice.

Silence.

Wendy: Just needs new wallpaper. And maybe a new bathroom. But apart from that... all good.

Silence. Stephanie eventually re-enters the room.

Stephanie: Right the soup is nearly ready, so why don't we take a seat and use this time to top up our glasses. After you.

After a long pause, Maria moves and sits down. Eventually, Abigail moves, followed by Sophia. Stephanie moves to an empty place and pulls out a chair.

Stephanie: This is your place Wendy.

Wendy: Thank you... very kind.

Wendy sits. When she has settled, Stephanie passes each lady a glass filled with wine. Whilst she does this, she speaks.

Stephanie: Oh how rude of me, I haven't introduced everyone to you. Wendy, this lovely lady next to you is Maria. And next to her is Abigail and at the end is Sophia.

Wendy: *(Still nervous)* Well it is really nice to meet you... really nice.

Stephanie: Well it is our pleasure.

Stephanie sits.

Stephanie: Right, I think a toast is in order. To our new friend Wendy. Welcome. We hope you enjoy your evening with us and find happiness in your new home. To Wendy.

Stephanie raises her glass. No one else moves.

Wendy: That is very nice of you, thank you.

Stephanie: Right... what shall we talk about?

Silence.

Stephanie: Oh I know... did I tell you all about Clara Perkins? No? Well, as you know, her husband often works away. Something to do with the government I think. Anyway, apparently Clara found a hotel receipt in his trouser pocket for a place in Yorkshire. Only problem is... he told her he was going to London. So, for peace of mind, she hired a private detective and lo and behold, three days later a stack of photographs land on her doorstep clearly showing Peter, her husband, and another woman in the middle of the act. Shocking stuff.

Silence.

Stephanie: Right, I'll just see how that soup is getting on.

Stephanie stands.

Wendy: Could I possibly use your bathroom before dinner Stephanie?

Stephanie: Of course dear. Right this way.

Wendy smiles at the others and follows Stephanie out of the room. As soon as she is gone the others come to life.

Maria: *(Panicking)* Oh my God, I don't believe this.

Sophia: Like I said, huge coincidence or cruel joke?

Abigail: *(Annoyed)* I don't believe in coincidences. I think someone is having a laugh at our expense.

Maria: *(Getting upset)* A laugh? This isn't a laugh. This is sick. A sick and twisted act.

Abigail: But why is Stephanie doing this? I mean, surely she knows how bad taste this is.

Sophia: I think she's lost the plot. You heard her earlier. Moving on and bringing in a replacement. She's up to something and I for one do not like being placed in this situation.

Maria: But it's uncanny. I mean *(Pause)* it could be her.

Abigail: But you know it can't be.

Maria: I know. *(Pause)* But she is the spitting image. Even down to her eye colour.

Sophia: I think tonight is a very elaborate hoax with very carefully planning.

Abigail: But why is she doing this? What is Stephanie getting from this farcical stunt?

Sophia: I don't know… but I'm going to find out.

Stephanie re-enters.

Stephanie: Well I hope you like carrot and coriander because I've made enough…

Stephanie notices that the other women are staring at her.

Stephanie: Is Wendy not back yet?

Sophia: *(Angry)* What the hell is going on Stephanie?

Stephanie: *(Confused)* I don't know what you mean?

Abigail: *(Angry)* You know exactly what we mean!

Stephanie: I'm sure I don't…

Sophia: When did you meet her? Where did you meet? And why have you brought her here?

Stephanie: Can somebody please let me in on the secret?

Abigail: Don't act dumb dear, it doesn't suit you.

Stephanie: *(Raising her voice)* You've all gone mad. Stark raving mad. And I will not be spoken to like this in my own home. So please kindly collect your coats and close the door on your way out.

Maria: No. *(Pause)* No way. You are going to answer our questions, because at this very moment I am freaking out and I will not be forced to relive what happened.

Silence.

Maria: *(Voice breaking)* She looks just like her.

Silence.

Maria: Don't make me say her name... please.

Silence.

Maria: Jennifer... she looks just like Jennifer.

Stephanie: *(Dismissive)* No, you're wrong She looks nothing like her.

Abigail: *(Raising her voice)* She looks the spitting image of her and you know it.

Sophia: So why is she here? Are you making fun of us?

Stephanie: *(Adamantly)* And why would I do that?

Abigail: Because you've clearly lost your mind.

Stephanie: *(Irate)* Remember whose house you are in Abigail.

Maria: You can't deny the similarities. Her face... her build... her height... even her eyes.

Stephanie: *(Patronizingly)* Now who's lost their mind?

Sophia: *(Shouting)* Don't patronise her. Tell us... is this supposed to be funny?

Stephanie: This is ridiculous. I have done nothing wrong. I was simply extending a hand of friendship to a lonely woman and now I am being attacked in my home. Well I won't have it. I won't have it. So please leave.

Maria: *(Starting to cry)* But she looks just like…

Stephanie: *(Shouting)* For goodness sake! Wendy looks nothing like Jennifer.

During the last few sentences of this argument, Wendy has (unseen by the others) re-entered the room.

Wendy: *(Confused)* Who's Jennifer?

All the women turn to face Wendy. They then look at each other in shock.

Flashback to 6 months earlier. The action changes into a happy, bubbly scene. All the women are chatting excitedly. Music plays and the women giggle and drink Champagne.

Maria: You have got to be joking.

Sophia: I swear it on my children's lives.

Jennifer: He actually said that to you? In front of all those people?

Sophia: He didn't say it… he shrieked it at the top of his voice.

The women laugh. Stephanie enters carrying a present.

Stephanie: And what are you four giggling at?

Abigail: Sophia is telling us about that young man from the supermarket.

Maria: He's been obsessed with her for years.

Sophia: *(Playfully dismissive)* I wouldn't say years.

Abigail: Well a long time anyway.

Stephanie: Why, what has he done?

Maria: *(Laughing)* He only went and shouted… no… shrieked that he loved her whilst she was down the frozen foods isle.

Stephanie: *(Shock)* No!

Sophia: I kid you not.

Jennifer: Well what did you do?

Sophia: What could I do? I simply paid for my ice-cream and left.

Abigail: He sounds like a loony.

Sophia: He looks like one too.

The women all laugh.

Stephanie: Anyway ladies, I'm just about to serve so if you'd like to take a seat at the table.

The ladies all move towards the table and begin to take their seats.

Maria: Is he the one with the rather large nose?

Abigail: And big ears.

Sophia: His ears are not that big.

Jennifer: I've seen this boy and let's just say that your Michael has nothing to worry about.

Jennifer goes to sit in the middle seat.

Stephanie: Oh Jennifer… I've set this seat out for you.

Stephanie stands next to the seat furthest to the right.

Jennifer: *(Puzzled)* Oh… OK.

Abigail: That's a curve ball Stephanie. We've sat in the same seats for the last four years.

Stephanie: I know. But Jennifer is the birthday girl and deserves top billing. Please… sit.

Jennifer looks at the others. The others look confused. Slowly Jennifer moves to her new seat.

Stephanie: Now… everyone else please.

The others slowly sit down.

Stephanie: Great. Now, as it's the first time we've been together for a few weeks I thought I'd make a little toast.

Abigail: *(Playfully mocking)* There's nothing little about your toasts Stephanie.

Stephanie: *(Giggling)* Now, now Abigail. Anyway, I just think it's important to mark this special occasion with a few words.

Sophia: *(Playfully mocking)* Well come on then dear. My stomach is beginning to growl.

Stephanie raises her glass.

Stephanie: To Sophia. A dear friend who has helped us all through troubled times with a wicked sense of humour and a soft shoulder to cry on.

Stephanie toasts Sophia. The others follow.

Sophia: How lovely *(To Abigail)* What does she want?

Stephanie: And to Abigail. Whenever I need a trustworthy, and sometimes brutal opinion, I turn to her. A friend whose tongue can only speak the truth and whose honesty does her great credit.

Stephanie toasts Abigail. The others follow.

Abigail: You're not dying are you?

Stephanie: And sweet, sweet Maria. Never before have I felt such kindness from another human being. Her soft and gentle nature has been of great comfort to us all in times of stress and pressure.

Stephanie toasts Maria. The others follow.

Maria: *(Getting upset)* Oh I think I'm filling up.

Stephanie: To my friends. I hope you all have a wonderfully pleasant evening.

Stephanie toasts again. She takes a drink from her glass. There is an awkward silence.

Jennifer: Don't I get a toast Stephanie? Or have I unknowingly offended you all?

Pause.

Stephanie: Of course you get a toast. In fact, I left yours to the end for a very special reason. Here.

Stephanie holds out a present.

Stephanie: Happy Birthday Jennifer.

Jennifer takes the present.

Jennifer: I don't know what to say. You really shouldn't have.

Sophia: We didn't.

Abigail: I thought we made an agreement not to do presents this year.

Stephanie: I know, I know, but today is a special birthday... isn't it Jennifer?

Jennifer: Is it?

Maria: Why? *(Playfully mocking)* You're not the big four-oh are you?

Jennifer: I certainly am not you cheeky mare.

Abigail: *(Playfully teasing)* Well that dress is a little frumpy.

Sophia: *(Playfully teasing)* Not to mention that eye shadow. Tragic.

Jennifer: *(Playfully offended)* Very charming.

Stephanie: Ignore them. This is just my little way of saying... well... of saying how much I think of you.

Jennifer: Well I am overwhelmed, really I am.

Maria: This is so exciting. Open the card first.

Jennifer opens the card. She stares at the front of the card.

Stephanie: Do you like it? I found it in that new shop on the high street.

Sophia: What is it?

Maria: Looks like some sort of beach.

Abigail: Bit of an odd picture for a birthday card.

Sophia: Which beach is it?

Stephanie: I'm not actually sure? Do you know Jennifer?

Pause.

Jennifer: *(Hesitantly)* Er… it's Brighton beach… I think.

Stephanie: Oh that's right, Brighton beach. I thought I'd seen it before. It was featured on that 'Relocation, Relocation' programme. I've never been before though. Have you Sophia?

Sophia: Don't think so. I'm not really a beach sort of person.

Abigail: Me neither. Although I have been to Scarborough once. Terrible day out.

Stephanie: Have you been Maria?

Maria: Yes I think so. When I was about four or five. My parents and I visited an elderly relative for a few days. Charming town if I remember rightly.

Stephanie: Sounds very nice. What about you Jennifer… *(Deliberately)* have you ever been?

Silence.

Sophia: *(Frustrated)* Oh please just answer her Jennifer. I am so hungry I might just have to eat my hand.

Pause.

Jennifer: *(Uneasy)* Yes… yes I've been to Brighton.

Stephanie: Lovely. Was it as a child or have you visited recently?

Pause.

Jennifer: *(Uneasy)* I don't remember. A while ago I think... but... I don't really know.

Maria: What does it say inside the card?

Stephanie: Yes... do read it Jennifer.

Jennifer slowly opens the card. She reads. There is a long pause.

Abigail: Well? What does it say?

Jennifer: Dear Jennifer. Happy Birthday. Love from Stephanie.

Sophia: *(Disappointed)* Is that it?

Stephanie: What more should a birthday card say?

Maria: Well I think it's a lovely gesture. Come on Jennifer open your present.

Jennifer: I might save it for later.

Abigail, Sophia and Maria all tell her to open the present.

Stephanie: The girls are right Jennifer... you should open it now.

Jennifer pauses before slowly opening the present. Abigail, Sophia and Maria watch in silence.

Stephanie: I hope you like it. Took me ages to find all the little details.

Jennifer finishes opening the present and holds a box.

Stephanie: Happy Birthday darling.

Jennifer opens the box. She takes out a piece of paper.

Abigail: What is it?

Maria: *(Confused)* Some sort of receipt.

Sophia: For what?

Stephanie: There's more. Have a look.

Stephanie looks at Maria. Maria looks into the box and takes out a small bottle of shampoo.

Maria: Shampoo. Looks like it's from a hotel.

Sophia: Have you booked her a spa weekend?

Maria takes out a photograph.

Maria: And a picture… of a bed.

Abigail: Let me see.

Abigail takes the picture from Maria.

Abigail: What is this Stephanie? Have you booked her a room somewhere?

Maria takes out a rose.

Maria: This is getting a bit strange.

Sophia: *(Frustrated)* And boring. Can somebody please tell us what all this stuff is?

Stephanie: Gladly. Jennifer… do you want to… or should I do the honours?

They all look at Jennifer. Pause.

Maria: Jennifer?

Silence.

Jennifer: *(Avoids eve contact with the others)* I'm so sorry.

Abigail: *(Confused)* For what?

Jennifer: It wasn't supposed to be like this.

Sophia: I'm still bored.

Stephanie: Well let me fill the ladies in on all the little details. The receipt you saw was for a hotel in Brighton where my husband took Jennifer, giving her a beautiful rose before taking her to bed for a night of wild and sordid passion. Of course, if you look through her gift further you'll find evidence of all the other times that she and Kevin have been together. There's a small hand towel from a guesthouse in Torquay, an empty

Champagne bottle from a picnic in Windermere and a pair of pearl earrings that he gave her for her birthday last year during a trip to Edinburgh.

Silence.

Stephanie: *(Overly friendly)* Happy Birthday Jennifer.

Silence.

Sophia: *(Shock)* Is this true?

Jennifer: If I can just have a minute to explain.

Abigail: *(Angry)* Oh you can have more than a minute. What the hell are you playing at?

Jennifer: It's not as sordid as Stephanie is making out.

Sophia: *(Raising her voice)* Trips to hotels? Secret picnics with Champagne? The whole thing sounds sordid to me.

Jennifer: *(Almost pleading)* We didn't mean for anyone to find out like this.

Abigail: You mean you didn't mean for anyone to find out at all!

Jennifer: No, it's not like that. Please, Maria, if I can just explain.

Maria: *(Offended)* Why do you think I'd even want to know?

Jennifer: Because you above anyone will understand.

Pause.

Maria: Me? *(Angry)* Don't you dare insinuate that you and I have anything in common.

Stephanie: *(Provokingly)* That sounds a bit like an insult, doesn't it Maria?

Jennifer: It wasn't meant as an insult.

Stephanie: To imply that you, an honorable, hard-working mother would have any similarities to *(With venom)* an old, haggard, two faced whore.

Abigail: *(Loudly)* And you still haven't explained anything.

Jennifer: *(Loudly)* Because nobody will give me a chance to speak.

Sophia: OK… OK everyone… it's time for a bit of silence. Our "friend" Jennifer is about to tell us why she has been having an affair with one of her best friend's husbands.

Silence.

Stephanie: *(Overly friendly)* The floor is yours darling.

Silence. Jennifer speaks slowly and carefully.

Jennifer: I haven't been happy for ages. In fact… I'm not sure I've ever been truly happy. My marriage has been failing for years and you all know it… you just never actually said it. Anyway… a few years ago things became worse. The night of our tenth wedding anniversary… Paul didn't even want a party… but by the end of the night he had so much alcohol inside him he seemed to forget what we were celebrating in the first place. And then it happened. We got into an argument and… he hit me. For the next few months it happened again… and again.

Silence.

Maria: *(Offended)* And why the hell do you think I'd understand that more than anyone else?

Jennifer: *(Bitterly)* Oh drop the act Maria. We all know what he did to you.

Maria: *(Shocked and puzzled)* What?

Jennifer: She told us all years ago.

Jennifer points at Stephanie.

Stephanie: She's lying.

Jennifer: Oh yeah? Well how would I know that your husband forced you to abort your baby?

Stephanie: Don't listen to her Maria.

Jennifer: *(With venom)* That's right. Your so-called best friend isn't such a good keeper of secrets.

Maria turns to Sophia and Abigail.

Maria: *(Voice breaking)* Is this true? Did she tell you?

Pause.

Abigail: *(Hesitantly)* Yes… yes she told us.

Maria: And did she tell you why?

Pause.

Sophia: *(Hesitantly)* She said something about… she said that you found out the baby had… problems.

Jennifer: *(Nastily)* And that your darling husband forced you to get rid of it.

Silence.

Maria: *(To Stephanie)* I trusted you.

Stephanie: *(Pleading)* Maria, she is twisting what happened.

Maria: *(Crying)* You knew how hard it was for me to talk about it.

Sophia: Maria, we have never told anyone else… honestly.

Jennifer: *(Scoffs)* Honestly? What do you know about being honest? You don't know the meaning of the word.

Sophia: *(Getting irate)* I beg your pardon?

Jennifer: Drop the act Sophia. We all know about what happened with you and your bother-in-law.

Sophia: *(Shouting)* You don't know anything.

Abigail: She does… I told her.

Sophia: *(Confused)* What?

Abigail: Well I might as well admit it, she's only going to tell you anyway.

Sophia: *(Angry)* How could you?

Abigail: *(Angry)* Oh don't act the innocent Sophia; I know you were the one who told people about my breakdown.

Maria: *(Confused)* What breakdown?

Pause.

Abigail: After Sarah was born I felt a bit… well… a bit down. I found I was drinking a bit too much and the doctor referred me… to the Harlington Ward. And before anyone asks the question, yes I mean the psychiatric Harlington ward. *(Raising her voice)* And I know you told the others because you were the only one I told. So please, less of the dramatics.

Silence.

Jennifer: *(Provokingly)* Looks like I'm not the only one with dark secrets.

Stephanie takes back control.

Stephanie: OK… it's true. Maybe some of us haven't been the best of friends lately. *(Deliberately)* But we have never… never… done anything to hurt one another. But she… she has crossed a line and we all know that what she has done is far worse than what anyone else has.

Pause.

Sophia: Stephanie's right. *(With disgust)* How could you do that… and with her husband?

Jennifer: *(Pleading)* I know it was wrong. I didn't plan for it to happen… he was just so nice to me.

Stephanie: *(Mockingly)* How beautiful.

Abigail: Maybe we should just all go home.

Maria: *(Shouting)* No… no one's going anywhere. Stephanie's

69

right... what some of you have done hasn't been great... *(With hatred in her voice)* but you... you disgust me.

Jennifer: *(Begging)* Maria, please...

Maria: How dare you try and make out like me losing my baby is like you shacking up with another woman's husband.

Stephanie: She's disgusting.

Maria: And do you know what... Jennifer... I have never broken a secret before... I am not like this lot who take people's trust and throw it away... I am a good person.

Jennifer: I know you are...

Maria: *(With hatred in voice)* But I want you to know this. I am gong to tell everyone what you've done. I am going to visit every shop... every café... every restaurant... every school... every park... everywhere with your picture and tell anyone who'll listen what a dirty, rotten, disgusting human being you are.

Silence.

Jennifer: If you do... I'll tell everyone about what he did to you... and your baby.

Silence.

Maria runs at Jennifer and grabs hold of her hair. Sophia and Abigail try hard to break up the fight.

Abigail: *(To Jennifer)* I think it's time you left.

Jennifer: I mean it. I'll tell everyone... about all of you... I'll tell them everything.

Sophia: *(Angry)* No you will not. Because if you do... you're dead.

Jennifer laughs.

Sophia: *(Furiously)* Don't you dare laugh at me.

Abigail: You spiteful bitch.

Jennifer: If a word of this gets out I promise I will ruin you… all of you.

Jennifer goes to leave.

Stephanie: Before you go Jennifer… are you not a bit interested to know how I found out about your sordid little affair?

Jennifer turns to face Stephanie.

Stephanie: He told me…he told me everything. In fact, he was the one who got all this stuff from your house. The rose… the pictures. And do you know why he told me? *(With venom)* Because he is disgusted with himself. He is disgusted that he could allow himself to go anywhere near such a vile… ugly… creature. His words, not mine.

Silence.

Jennifer: I don't believe you.

Stephanie: You don't? Oh that's too bad. *(Enjoying the moment)* Can I ask, when was the last time you saw him? A week ago? Two weeks ago? And when was the last time he returned one of your calls? Or your emails? Or your text messages?

Silence.

Stephanie: *(Mockingly)* He told me everything because he loves me *(With hatred)* and he hates himself for touching you.

Silence.

Stephanie: *(Changing from nasty to polite)* It was so lovely of you to come around tonight. We must do this again sometime.

Jennifer turns to leave.

Maria: I mean it Jennifer… everyone will find out about this.

Abigail: She's right. People are going to hate you for what you've done.

Sophia: How could you Jennifer... we're supposed to be your friends.

Maria: Ha... friends. She is no friend of mine... in fact... *(With pure and honest anger)* I wish you were dead.

At this point we fast forward back to the present day.

Wendy: *(Confused)* Who's Jennifer?

Silence.

Wendy: *(Getting more determined)* Who's Jennifer?

Stephanie: *(Casually)* Just an old friend.

Sophia: That's not strictly true.

Wendy: Which bit?

Abigail: Any of it.

Pause.

Maria: *(Hesitantly)* Jennifer was the woman who... well she was the woman who used to join us for dinner parties... before you.

Wendy: Oh.

Stephanie: *(Overly polite)* But we'd much rather have you here, wouldn't we ladies?

Sophia: *(Blankly)* If I had to choose then yes, I suppose we would.

Wendy: *(Cautiously)* And can I ask why Jennifer no longer comes to your dinner parties?

Silence.

Wendy: I take it she isn't invited anymore?

Abigail: *(Sarcastically)* Well if she was then we would need a Ouija board to ask her.

Pause.

Maria: *(Softly)* Jennifer's dead… she died about six months ago.

Abigail: And the thing is Wendy… the reason why we all seem a little shocked is… well, you and Jennifer… you look exactly the same.

Stephanie: *(Mockingly)* Exactly the same?

Abigail: *(Raising her voice)* OK you look similar.

Sophia: Very similar.

Maria: It's true. Look at this photo.

Maria goes to her handbag.

Abigail: *(Confused)* You keep a picture of her?

Sophia: That is pretty twisted Maria.

Maria passes the picture to Wendy.

Silence.

Maria: Do you see what we mean?

Wendy: Yes… yes I do. *(To Stephanie)* Is this why you invited me tonight?

Stephanie: What? Of course not. I don't think you look a thing like her.

Sophia: *(Irate)* Oh give it up Stephanie.

Abigail: *(Irate)* And start telling us what the hell is going on here.

Stephanie: Nothing is going on.

Wendy: How did she die?

Pause.

Wendy: Come on you must remember, how did she die?

Pause.

Maria: *(Carefully)* Do you want the official version… or the truth?

Wendy looks at Maria with confusion and fear.

Maria: Officially… she took an overdose… her husband found her in the bath.

Pause.

Wendy: And the truth?

Pause.

Maria: *(Voice breaking)* I can't say it.

Stephanie: *(Bluntly)* We killed her. Is that what you are getting Maria?

Wendy: *(Shocked)* What?

Stephanie: *(Bluntly)* Yes, we all found out that Jennifer was a liar and a cheat and we threatened to expose her to the world. She panicked, went home and took a load of pills. Officially she committed suicide but stupid Maria believes we pushed her.

Maria: *(Crying)* We did push her!

Stephanie: *(Nastily)* She got what she deserved.

Abigail: That is going too far Stephanie.

Stephanie: *(Spitefully)* No one is asking for your opinion Abigail.

Sophia: But it's the truth.

Stephanie: The truth? *(Pause)* We were the ones who were going to expose the truth.

Abigail: Do you not think she suffered enough?

Sophia: *(Raising her voice)* The woman's dead, for God's sake.

Stephanie: And am I supposed to feel some sort of sympathy for her?

Maria: I didn't know you could be so heartless.

Stephanie: *(Coldly)* It wasn't your husband she was sleeping with.

Maria: *(Crying and shouting)* No but she'd be alive today if it was.

Stephanie: *(Shouting)* And what is that supposed to mean?

Sophia: Maria's right. If you hadn't been so intent on destroying her.

Stephanie: What, you mean like she destroyed my family?

Abigail: But your family are still alive.

Stephanie: *(Sarcastically)* And I'm supposed to thank her for that?

Sophia: *(Angry)* You planned all of this. You're not right in the head Stephanie.

Maria: She's right. I think you need help.

Stephanie: *(Sarcastically)* Oh thank you for the diagnosis.

Wendy: I think I should leave.

Stephanie: No… you are going nowhere Jennifer!

Stephanie grabs hold of Wendy's arm.

Silence.

Wendy: Jennifer?

Stephanie: I mean Wendy… I mean… you are going nowhere Wendy.

Pause.

Abigail: *(Bluntly)* Stephanie… you do realise that this woman is not Jennifer… don't you?

Pause.

Sophia: *(Scared and confused)* Her name is Wendy. You invited her. You told us her name was Wendy.

Pause.

Maria walks towards Stephanie. She takes her hand.

Maria: *(Softly)* Stephanie... look at me... this woman is not Jennifer. Her name is Wendy and she lives across the street.

Stephanie: *(Showing a vulnerable side)* I just thought... if we could find a replacement...

Maria: I know...

Stephanie: *(Voice breaking)* If we could just find someone to be like her then it's like it never happened... like Jennifer is still here.

Maria: *(Softly)* But Stephanie... this woman is not Jennifer. Jennifer is not here anymore... do you understand that?

Pause.

Wendy: I want to leave.

Stephanie: *(Suddenly snaps)* No! Nobody is leaving. Let's start again. Come on, right, Sophia you sit here and Abigail you're here and sweet Maria you're at the end and Jennifer is opposite me. Right who's for a glass of wine? Come on Jennifer, surely you'll have a drink with me, won't you? Now, what's the latest gossip? Come on, somebody get the ball rolling. Anyone? OK, I'll start. Did I tell you about the new couple who've moved in to the Johnsons' old place? Well apparently she is a doctor and he is a househusband? I mean, have you ever heard of anything so silly? A househusband?

During the above speech Stephanie tries to look as normal as possible as the others watch her in horror.

Stephanie: Well come on then, sit down. The soup will go cold if we don't eat it now.

Nobody moves.

Stephanie: Sit down ladies... I won't ask you again.

Nobody moves.

Stephanie: *(Turning sinister)* If I'm honest you're all making me a little mad… please.

Slowly all the ladies sit down.

Stephanie: *(Overly friendly)* Good. Now, this couple who've moved in to the Johnsons' have two children but the rumour is that the older one isn't his. But don't ask where I heard that because my lips are sealed. The younger one is a musician, piano I think. Apparently she's tipped to be a real star of the future but you know what people say, parents believe their children can do anything.

As Stephanie is reciting this last speech the lights fade.

The End

Have You Seen Down There Lately?

Synopsis

Set in a 21st century office, God and her three angels meet to discuss the declining number of believers. Led by Gabrielle, the angels try and convince their leader that they need to modernise their ways if they are to have any chance of attracting the younger generation. However, persuading God to leave behind her tried and tested methods might be easier said than done.

Character Description

God – The head of the 'business'. She needs thoroughly convincing if she is to make any big decisions. God can appear moody and even stubborn.

Gabrielle – God's 'right-hand woman'. She is the 'project manager' and likes to remain in control of the group. Gabrielle can become frustrated at others, especially if they are side-tracked or fall off task.

Michaela and Raquel – Unlike Gabrielle they are not fully committed to work. They seek easy answers and are quick to shift any blame that comes their way. Michaela and Raquel appear like a double act.

Original Staging

Setting: Office.

Audience: End-on theatre (forward facing audience).

Set: Chairs (bigger chair for God), table, two flip charts.

Props: Pens, paper, cups, coffee pot.

Costume: Either typical office wear (suits) or typical biblical wear (or a mixture of the two).

NB: *With some slight editing this play could be altered to accommodate male actors.*

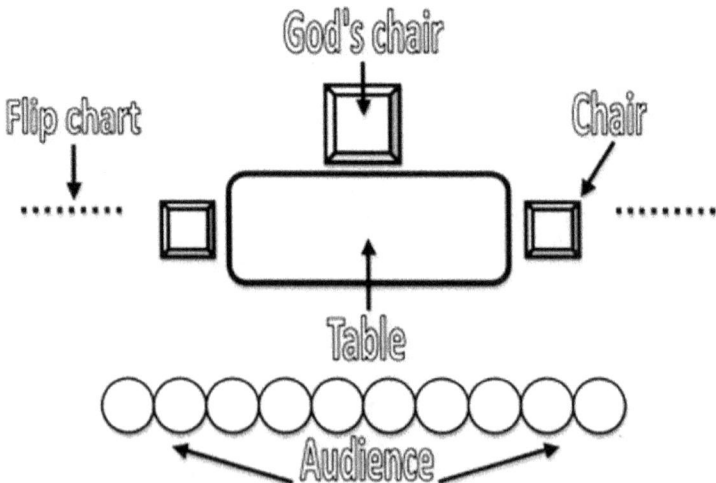

Have You Seen Down There Lately?

God is sat at the middle point of a large table with her back to the audience. Michaela is also sat at the table. Gabrielle is stood looking at a flip chart. Raquel is pouring coffee from a pot

Gabrielle: *(Puzzled)* It just doesn't add up… we've never put in as many hours but the numbers just keep dropping.

Michaela: Maybe the data is wrong.

Raquel: *(Abruptly)* Excuse me! I checked and re-checked that data at least five times.

Michaela: *(Provokingly)* Well maybe you made a mistake…

Raquel: *(Getting annoyed)* I don't make mistakes.

Gabrielle: Well something isn't right. What if we do another sweep, see if anything has improved?

God: *(Calmly)* That won't be necessary.

Raquel: But it might help if…

God: It won't help…

Michaela: But…

God: It won't… help.

Silence.

Gabrielle: But that means, if the information we have is correct, the only reason for such a low turnout is… well… is…

God: A lack of faith?

God slowly turns around to face the others.

God: Ladies, my problem is not the empty churches.

Raquel: *(Confused)* Not a problem?

Michaela: Bums on seats. It's what it's all about.

Gabrielle: It's what we need to survive.

81

God: *(Raising her voice)* Silence… *(Calmer tone)* Empty churches are the least of our worries… it's the people, they are the concern.

Michaela: The people?

God: People do not believe any more, they do not have faith. This lack of belief has led to a decline in standards. Basic moral standards.

Raquel: *(Directly)* It is more than basic morals.

Gabrielle: Things have become much worse in recent times.

God: But things are retrievable.

Raquel: *(Scoffs)* Are they?

God: Of course.

Silence.

Michaela considers what she is about to say.

Michaela: Have you… seen down there lately?

God: *(Angry tone)* What are you insinuating? That I have forgotten my duties? That I have abandoned the people who need me most?

Michaela: *(Panicking)* That's not what I'm saying at all…

God: Then what are you saying?

Gabrielle jumps in to save to situation.

Gabrielle: I think Michaela just means that times have changed. And you do have a tendency to see the best in a bad situation.

God: And this is a crime?

Gabrielle: Not at all. But maybe now is not the time to be positive… but to be realistic.

Raquel flips the chart to show problems in the world.

Raquel: Look at the modern world. It's full of disaster and death and disease.

God: But it is also full of hope and happiness and humanity.

Gabrielle: But that is only in a minority of cases, the masses have slipped.

Michaela: Gabrielle is right. The dedication of our small group of followers will never wane. But you have to admit… we have lost a lot recently.

Silence.

God takes a big intake of breath.

God: You're right. I know you're right. I was hoping that this was just a blip. I mean, people have got things wrong in the past.

Raquel seizes the moment to agree with God.

Raquel: Of course, I still remember the witch trials.

Michaela: And Hitler. He was wrong on many levels.

Gabrielle: But with all due respect; I don't think this blip is going to go away in the near future.

Pause.

God: So what do we do?

Raquel: *(Proudly)* Well, we have been working on a few things. What about this… a miracle?

God looks at Raquel in confusion.

God: A miracle?

Raquel: Yeah, a miracle always helps to rekindle lost faith.

Michaela: Raquel is right. It doesn't have to be anything major. You know, a disabled child walks again.

Raquel: Or a man survives after falling from a six storey building. Something that the tabloids would lap up.

Pause.

God: *(Incredulously)* And how would that help to cure

people's lack of faith?

Awkward silence.

Raquel: *(Hesitantly)* It's a miracle. People love miracles.

Gabrielle: OK, maybe that's not the answer. But we need to act now, before it's too late.

Pause. God rubs her face, showing how stressful she is finding this situation.

God: You're right. OK, let me think. We need to halt this decline in standards… and it is proven that a strong belief system is key to good moral beings… but to have faith we must first remind them that there is something to believe in.

The next three lines are delivered with a quick pace.

Michaela: *(Triumphantly)* Excellent.

God: You need to pay them a visit.

Michaela: *(Shocked)* What?

Raquel: *(Panicking)* You can not be serious. You can't possibly want us to enter such an inhospitable environment.

God: *(Dismissive)* It is not an inhospitable environment.

Gabrielle: I'm afraid it is. Do you not remember that last time we went down there?

Michaela: I was heckled because of my pale complexion and poor Gabrielle was labelled with many a derogatory term.

Raquel: "Gay lord", "Gay lover"…

Gabrielle: *(Embarrassed)* Thank you Raquel.

Michaela flips the chart over again.

Michaela: The point is it's not safe for us. *(She indicates images as she mentions them)* Hoodies roam the streets looking for trouble. Knife and gun crime is at an all time high. Drug and alcohol abuse is a widespread problem. To send us down there is like committing professional… and actual… suicide.

God: *(Getting annoyed)* And staying up here and doing nothing is a better option?

Raquel: Well what about if we sent someone else down.

God: *(Confused)* Someone else?

Raquel: Yes. Someone who can rejuvenate the masses, get them enthusiastic about faith… make them believe again.

God: We have tried that before and it did not work.

Raquel: But is it not worth another try?

God: *(Loudly)* No! And I will not discuss this option any further. *(Calmer tone)* Now if you will excuse me I need a short toilet break.

God exits.

Michaela: Who else did we send down there?

Gabrielle: Please tell me you are joking.

Michaela: What?

Gabrielle: You don't remember the last time we sent a man down there to spread God's message?

Michaela: No, should I?

Gabrielle: You don't remember a man performing miracles and sacrificing himself so he could make the world a better place?

Silence.

Michaela: *(Hesitantly)* Err… yeah of course I do… ha, ha, I'm joking, just pulling your leg.

Raquel whispers to Michaela.

Raquel: Do you really know who she's on about?

Michaela: *(Whispering)* Haven't got a clue… have you?

Raquel: Not the foggiest!

Gabrielle: So now what? We need to think of something, the boss has never looked so stressed.

Michaela: Deadlines are a bugger aren't they?

Raquel: *(Defiantly)* Well whatever it is, I am not going down there again.

Michaela: Are things really so bad? I mean, yes, numbers are down, but we are not in any mortal danger are we?

Gabrielle is beginning to get frustrated and angry.

Gabrielle: We might not be, but they are killing each other as we speak. No, we need to act now and fast.

God enters. Raquel does not see her.

Raquel: *(Excited)* I've got it!

God: Yes.

Raquel panics.

Raquel: Err... no it doesn't matter; it's not a great idea really.

God: Well any idea is better than no idea, so let's hear it.

Raquel: I really don't think you'll like it.

God: *(Slightly threatening)* Tell me!

Silence.

Raquel: *(Hesitantly)* OK... well... as you know, the last time we paid them a visit it was an unmitigated disaster, an absolute debacle, an incredible...

God: *(Angry)* Get on with it!

Raquel: Well, what if instead of us going down there... err... you went?

God is shocked at Raquel's suggestion.

God: Me?

Gabrielle: *(Disbelievingly)* You must be joking?

Raquel: Why?

God: You think I should go down there?

Gabrielle: *(Getting angry)* You have had some bad ideas in the past but this one takes the biscuit.

Raquel: *(Defiantly)* But she's the one they want to see.

Things have escalated in to an argument.

Gabrielle: A minute ago you were telling us how dangerous things are down there...

Raquel: Well they are...

Gabrielle: So you want to send her instead...

Raquel: Well I don't see you coming up with any ideas...

Gabrielle: That's because I am trying to think of something remotely achievable...

God: *(Very loud)* SILENCE! *(Pause)* I need some time to think.

Silence.

Michaela tries to salvage the situation.

Michaela: What if you didn't actually go down there... but you made an appearance in another form.

Gabrielle: Another form?

Michaela: Yeah. Remember, we've done it before. We just leave her image in a convenient place and let one of them find it.

Gabrielle: Where?

Michaela: *(Childishly)* Oh I don't know. Do I have to think of everything? On a piece of toast or a Pop Tart.

Raquel: Oh yeah. Last time we left it on an oil patch in Coventry.

Gabrielle: And how would that help?

Michaela: People see it, tell the papers, they take photos and make up stories which lead to a rise in people believing, which in turn leads to an increase in moral standards.

Raquel: *(Impressed)* That is brilliant.

Michaela: *(Pleased with herself)* Thanks, I just thought of it.

Raquel: What just now?

Michaela: Yeah.

God interrupts and ends the positive feeling.

God: No. No more gimmicks. No more quick fixes. We have to think about the long-term future of this world. Putting my picture on a hot cross bun won't work.

Michaela: *(Immaturely)* Actually it was a Pop Tart.

God: It won't work.

Silence.

Gabrielle: I agree. I think we need to make some drastic changes.

Raquel: Changes?

Gabrielle: We need to look at ourselves and what we can change to solve this crisis.

Raquel: *(Whispering to Michaela)* What does she mean by changes?

Michaela: *(Whispering to Raquel)* I don't know but I've got my union on speed dial if they try anything funny.

God: What do you have in mind?

Gabrielle: Well, what I'm going to propose is pretty radical.

Pause.

God: Go on.

Gabrielle: It seems to me that if we are to change we need to first highlight the main issue that needs to be addressed.

Raquel jumps in, quickly followed by Michaela.

Raquel: It's got to be Hoodies…

Michaela: No it's rising petrol prices, cost me a fortune to get here…

Raquel: And congestion doesn't help…

Michaela: No it doesn't…

Gabrielle: *(Loudly)* Please, will you just stop… sorry, where was I? Oh yes, the issue that we need to address must be the youth, the younger generation. If we can get them to believe that will have a knock-on effect with future generations.

God: But we have discussed this before. The young do not want to concern themselves with our values; it is simply a lost cause.

Gabrielle: *(Hesitantly)* But, if I may be so bold as to say, our last attempt to convert them was a little… well… weak.

God: *(Insulted)* And you have a better idea?

Gabrielle: Well actually, *we* have had a better idea.

God: *(Surprised)* We?

Raquel tries to back out and is quickly backed up by Michaela.

Raquel: Gabrielle, I'm not sure this will work…

Michaela: Raquel's right, let's discuss this later… does anyone want another coffee?

Gabrielle: We had a meeting last night.

Pause.

God: Last night?

Gabrielle: Yes. I'm sorry for not informing you but it was very last minute.

Michaela: *(Creeping)* I did say we should have called you.

God: And what were the findings of this… meeting?

Gabrielle: We feel that the world has moved at such a rapid pace recently. Times have changed, people, and more importantly, technology has developed... improved.

God: Well I feel that we have made a conscious effort to keep up.

Gabrielle: Have we?

Raquel: *(Hesitantly)* Gabrielle has a point... you haven't even got email.

God: Emails are so impersonal. The people can still contact me using a good old fashion prayer.

Gabrielle: But the younger generation don't use prayers, they use email.

Michaela: Or text message. Although, if we did start using text message I'd be useless. They shorten the words and use numbers instead of letters. It gets me ever so confused.

God: *(Firmly)* We won't be using text message or email.

Raquel: What about fax?

God: *(Firmly)* Or fax!

Gabrielle: But we need to move in to the twenty-first century. Prayers and church visits are no longer appropriate; we need to reach them in other ways.

God feels insulted.

God: And what do you suggest?

Raquel: For years, the young have been using something called 'The World Wide Web', also known as 'The Internet'.

God: I have heard of 'The Internet' thank you Raquel.

Raquel: Ah, but have you heard of the benefits of using this ingenious invention?

Michaela: The Web is used by a significant number of the world's population. In their homes, their work places, even on the high street.

Raquel: People can 'log on' almost anywhere. We propose that we use this popular manner of communication to reach the masses.

Michaela: We reach them through web pages. You know, get them to leave messages on your MySpace page or become a friend on Facebook.

God: *(Confused)* My face on what space?

Raquel: It's perfect.

Gabrielle: What do you think?

Pause.

God takes a long look at her co-workers.

God: So you want me to agree to abandon tried and tested methods of prayer in favour of new and complicated technology… I love it!

Raquel: Really?

Michaela: *(Excited)* Yes! This is it! We're on the way back to the top.

Michaela and Raquel celebrate. Gabrielle tries to calm the situation down.

Gabrielle: There is one other change we could make?

Raquel tries to change the conversation.

Raquel: Leave it Gabrielle.

Michaela: Yeah, let's just see if this works first.

Gabrielle: We agreed, it's all of nothing.

God: All of nothing? What else is there to change?

Silence.

Gabrielle: You.

God: Me?

Raquel: Oh she's done it now!

God: What do I need to change?

Gabrielle: Well, your image is a bit… well… dated.

God: *(Offended)* Dated?

Michaela: *(Creeping)* In a good way!

Gabrielle: As the world has changed… you have not.

God: Well, I have to agree I am not exactly a trendsetter but I fail to see what this has to do with improving moral standards.

Gabrielle: Well actually… it has everything to do with the world's morals. Raquel!

Raquel flips the chart as she speaks.

Raquel: You see, the youth of today are an impressionable group. And they are influenced not by faith but by culture, and in particular the celebrity culture. Out are the days of God and worship and in is the time of Victoria Beckham and Gucci.

Michaela: The young adore Mrs. Beckham.

Raquel: Gabrielle feels…

Gabrielle: *(Annoyed)* Raquel!

Raquel: OK… we feel that to really engage the younger generation we need to mix with their way of life.

God: And how do we do that?

Michaela: Ah, we are glad you asked, please observe. Firstly we need to get your name known again, put God back on the map. We need to advertise that fact that you are making a comeback.

God: *(Confused)* A comeback? But I've never been away!

Gabrielle: It would be marketed very tactfully…

God: *(Confused)* Marketed?

The next section of dialogue is delivered quickly. Its aim is to bamboozle God.

Gabrielle: We could start with a small slot between Coronation Street and...

Raquel: Or Deal or No Deal...

Michaela: I love that programme...

God: *(Confused)* I don't get it... what are we advertising?

Pause.

Gabrielle: You.

Michaela: We've already devised some tag lines. How about this one... 'The God Squad'.

God: *(Confused)* The God Squad?

Michaela: Yeah, it's kind of like 'Waking the Dead' but instead of her from the 'Royle Family' it's you and other biblical characters.

Raquel: How about this for a first episode... Murder on the Ark.

Michaela: Two innocent little sheep murdered and you have to solve the crime.

God: *(Confused)* What?

Raquel: Or 'God's Saturday Night Take Away'. A family show where you and a designated sidekick have fun and frolics...

Michaela: We've already lined up Kelly Osborne to be your partner...

God: *(Loudly and directly)* Just stop this, stop this right now!

Pause.

Gabrielle: Something the matter?

God: Yes, this is preposterous. Crime shows, family entertainment, I don't see how this is going to help our cause.

Raquel: This bit won't.

God looks puzzled and bewildered.

Gabrielle: No, this is just about raising your profile. Once people know who you are again they will no doubt want to know more about you.

Michaela: That's when I call in a favour from my editor friend at 'Hello' magazine.

God puts her head in her hands.

God: Please tell me you are joking.

Michaela: Oh no. It is proven that any celebrity that appears in this magazine has influence and power over the youth today.

God: *(Exasperated)* How? How is that at all possible?

Raquel: Did you ever hear of Amy Winehouse? Well, she was a pretty average celebrity. She had a good singing voice but for some reason her music wasn't selling. So, her publicist arranged for her to be photographed doing things she shouldn't be... then she became a Grammy award winning artist with millions of adoring fans.

God: So what are you saying? That I need to photographed... doing drugs!

Gabrielle: *(Back tracking)* Oh my word no, not at all, we would never dream of asking you to do that.

God breathes a sign of relief.

Gabrielle: But you will need to attend a few film premieres, and possibly with a good-looking man on your arm.

God: *(Incensed)* What! No way! Not a chance! I do not want to listen to this anymore!

Michaela: But...

God: No buts! Just listen to what you're asking me to do. You want me to star in adverts to promote my crime show which will lead to people wanting to know more about me which in turn leads to my appearance in a celebrity magazine with some strange man on my arm! What next? A reality show?

Raquel: Err… no… of course not.

Raquel quickly turns over the flip chart to hide the page saying 'I'm A Religious Figure… Get Me Out Of Here'.

Gabrielle: But this is what they want now. There is no other way to reach them.

Silence.

Gabrielle: OK… what if we don't use the TV ideas.

Michaela: *(Disappointed)* Gabrielle!

Gabrielle: Just hear me out… what if we don't use the TV ideas but we do advertise the fact that you have changed.

Pause.

God: Go on.

Gabrielle: Well look at Madonna… her music is pretty average.

Raquel: *(Offended)* That might be your opinion.

Gabrielle: But she simply reinvents herself, changes her looks to keep up with today's culture. If we did the same with you it might have a significant impact.

Silence.

God: Continue.

Gabrielle: Excellent… Michaela.

Michaela begins to turn the flip chart.

Michaela: OK. To reinvent is to modernise. At present you appear to be old and tired. So we have come up with a few ways for you to appeal to the young. How about this… Stylish God.

Raquel: Stylish God looks great in this little black dress with matching handbag. Notice how the shoes help to elongate the legs.

God: *(Unconvinced)* Mmmm!

Gabrielle: OK, try this next one.

Raquel: WAG God. Football has never been so big.

God: No chance!

Gabrielle: OK, I am confident you will love this next one.

Raquel: God... the sex symbol.

God: Next!

Raquel: But sex sells.

God has finally reached saturation point.

God: Stop this, please stop this at once. I've had enough. I can not stand this nonsense. Dressing me up as a footballer or sex slave...

Gabrielle: *(Trying to convince)* But we need to act now, you said so yourself.

God: I know what I said but this is all useless. The emails, the TV shows, the reinventing, it is not what we need.

Gabrielle: Numbers are dropping as we speak.

God: Well good, let them!

The others gasp in horror.

God's last speech is delivered with passion.

God: Maybe we are focusing too much on those who do not believe and not those who do. Ladies, do not misunderstand me, I wish this world was a better place, truly I do, but maybe we just have to accept the fact that people are too busy to care about us and our morals. I propose that we abandon all these silly ideas of modernisation. We do not need to prove ourselves to anyone. We just need to be here if and when they call upon us for help. Surely we can provide this? And if people don't ask for assistance maybe they do not need it. But people will always need someone to turn to… in times of trouble; they will always need someone to talk to. We can still be those people. Please, ladies, I thank you for your efforts but I believe our work for tonight is done. But I can assure you… we will always have a role to play for the people.

The End

Three Mothers

Synopsis

Whilst waiting for a flu injection, three mothers-to-be sit in a doctor's surgery and discuss a variety of topics, in particular the failings of men. However, as their conversations develop, it is revealed that the three women have more in common than just being pregnant.

Character Description

Debs – The typical 'rough' woman. She is loud, crude and not afraid to speak her mind. Debs hates being looked down on, which puts her at odds with Claudia.

Claudia – The typical 'upper-class' woman. She dislikes having to be in a waiting room with people like Debs and does her best to avoid engaging in any conversations. However, as the play develops we see her 'perfect' life is far from ideal.

Abby – The young one. Waiting to have an injection scares Abby but not as much as the thought of giving birth and raising a child alone. She is nervous and vulnerable and likely to burst into tears at any moment.

Original Staging

Setting: A doctor's waiting room.

Audience: End-on theatre (forward facing audience).

Set: Chairs.

Props: Three mobile phones.

Costume: Everyday clothes, pregnancy bumps.

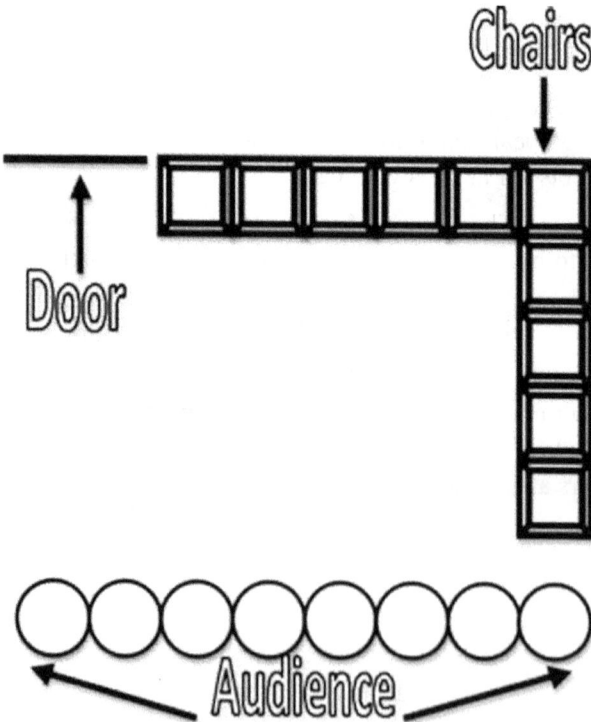

Three Mothers

The waiting room of a doctors' surgery. Claudia is looking through some leaflets. She is heavily pregnant. As she goes to sit she notices the chair is dirty. She takes out a handkerchief and dusts down the chair. She is not happy with the result so she places the cloth on the seat and sits down.

Debs enters. She is also heavily pregnant.

Debs: *(Shouting back through the door)* Load of shit, absolute load of shit. If she thinks I'm waiting around for more than five minutes she's got another think coming. Bloody joke it is, a bloody joke. I mean, it's not my fault the taxi didn't turn up is it? I can't help it if I got up late and missed the bus is it? A bloody joke.

Claudia has slightly turned her body away from Debs.

Debs: What time you in?

Claudia: Pardon?

Debs: *(Slowly)* What time… you in?

Claudia: *(Confused)* In? In where?

Debs: In there. What time are you in there?

Claudia: Oh my appointment. Oh not till half past.

Debs: *(Scoffs)* Half past? Bloody hell you're a bit keen aren't you? Only just gone ten to.

Claudia: Well I like to be early.

Debs: Me too. I planned to be early this morning but had a right nightmare with our Wayne last night. He rolls in at four this morning… drunk as a skunk. I said to him I said *(Shouting)* "Oi, you little bastard! I've got a bloody appointment in the morning so keep the bloody noise down," and he just turns around and says *(Shouting)* "Oh stop shouting woman, I'm trying to…"

Claudia: Sorry can you just excuse me. I have to make a call.

Claudia moves away from Debs and pulls out her mobile phone. Abby enters looking very worried. Like the other two women, she is also heavily pregnant.

Debs: You here for your jab love?

Abby: *(Confused)* What?

Debs: Swine flu. Are you here for your swine flu jab?

Abby: *(Nervously)* Oh… yeah, yeah, the nurse said to wait in here.

Debs: Well I just told her I'm not waiting more than five minutes. I mean it's not my fault the taxi didn't turn up is it, or I got up late and missed the bus is it? Bloody typical though, I don't know why I'm surprised.

Claudia: *(Talking into her phone)* Darling… it's me… yes I'm in the waiting room now.

Debs: What time you in?

Abby: Ten past.

Claudia: *(Talking in to her phone)* What time are you going to get here?…

Debs: She's not in till half past. I said to her I said "Bit keen aren't you?"…

Claudia: *(Talking in to her phone – sounding hurt)* But you promised…

Abby: *(Anxiously)* I just wanna get this over with.

Debs: Aw… scared of needles? Trust me love. After childbirth, nothing scares you any more.

Claudia: *(Talking in to her phone - pleading)* Darling… please… I need you…

Debs: It was the most painful thing ever. *(Exaggerates the next* *word)* Ever!

Claudia: *(Talking in to her phone)* OK... well will I see you later?

Debs: Like pushing a bowling ball through a polo.

Claudia: *(Talking in to her phone)* OK well... darling... darling... are you there... hello... hello...

Debs: *(To Claudia)* Signal's crap in here love.

Claudia: What?

Debs: Won't even let you send a text. But don't bother asking her out there to use the phone. *(Shouts)* Emergency only!

Claudia sits down and stares at her mobile.

Debs: I don't know why we're bothering with this needle anyway. I heard that people are dropping dead after they've had it.

Abby: *(Panicking)* What? Is that true?

Debs: *(Causally)* Oh yeah. I saw it on the telly just the other night. Young girl, healthy as anything. Needle. Dead.

Abby: Oh I don't need this.

Abby puts her head in her hands.

Claudia: *(Directly)* That's nonsense.

Debs: *(Offended)* You what?

Claudia: Absolute nonsense.

Debs: Err... what do you mean absolute nonsense?

Claudia: There is no evidence that this swine flu jab can be fatal. In fact, a recent study...

Debs: A recent study? *(Mockingly)* What are you, a professor or something?!

Claudia: A recent study showed that the benefits of having the H1N1 Influenza injection far out weigh any potential risk.

Abby: How do you know?

Claudia: My husband…

Debs: *(Loudly)* Well I'm just saying what our Joanne told me and she knows a guy who drinks in her pub that used to work with a woman whose brother was a doctor.

Claudia: Well I'm sure he was mistaken.

Debs: *(Calmly tone)* Yeah maybe. He ain't a doctor anymore. Got fired for touching up women.

Abby: *(Fighting back tears)* I hate this. Can they not hurry it up?

Claudia: *(Reassuringly)* I'm sure they won't be long.

Silence.

Debs: *(Trying to get a conversation started)* Bloody men!

Silence.

Debs: I tried to get mine to come with me today but he wouldn't shift his arse.

Silence.

Debs: You can't rely on a bloke can you?

Silence

Debs: *(To Claudia)* Your fella not wanna come either?

Claudia: *(Trying to avoid talking to Debs)* No… well he wanted to but… well he's working, so…

Debs: Yeah mine too. Well, not actually working but… yeah.

Silence.

Debs: Yours working too love?

Abby: I don't know. Probably.

Debs: Aw… where does he work?

Abby: *(Hesitantly)* I… don't know…

Debs: You don't know?

Abby: *(Nervously)* I... he works... used to work... I don't know...

Claudia: You don't have to answer if you don't want to.

Debs: *(Offended)* Ay... do you mind? We're having a conversation here.

Claudia: *(Directly)* The girl clearly does not want to discuss the father of her child.

Debs: *(Raising her voice)* She'll tell me if she wants to.

Claudia: *(Raising her voice)* Well I don't think she wants to.

Debs: You don't know that!

Claudia: I have a feeling that I do.

Debs: *(Spitefully)* Oh I know your type. Snooty like. Always looking down your nose at people, thinking you're always right.

Claudia: (*Laughing)* Considering we have only just met that is a very inaccurate and unflattering assumption you have just made.

Debs: *(Getting angry)* I can make unflattering assumptions whenever I like. I can also talk to anyone I like and I wanna talk to her. *(To Abby)* So, as I was saying before I was rudely interrupted...

Abby: *(Shouting)* I don't know who the dad is.

Silence.

Abby: *(Calmer)* I mean... I think I know but... well he can't be, so...

Claudia: You don't need to say any more.

Pause.

Debs: *(With disgust)* The dirty slapper!

Claudia: *(Incensed)* You can't say that!

Debs: No wonder this country is going down the bog.

Claudia: Please just ignore her.

Debs: And to not even know who the kid's dad is!

Claudia: *(Fighting back)* And I suppose you have never made a mistake?

Debs: Not like her. I know who's the dad of every one of my kids.

Claudia: *(Raising her voice)* Oh I suppose having children with different men is better?

Debs: *(Raising her voice)* Much better than stopping a baba seeing their dad.

Silence. Debs sits away from the others.

Claudia: *(To Abby)* Are you OK? Just ignore her, she's… well… common.

Abby: *(Fighting back the tears)* I do know who the dad is but… he's married.

Claudia: Does he know? About the baby?

Abby: I told him but. And he says he loves me but doesn't want anything to do with his son.

Claudia: You're having a boy?

Abby: Yeah. I've not even told my parents.

Claudia: But surely they've guessed already.

Abby: I don't see them very much. In fact… not since Christmas.

Claudia: *(Sympathetically)* You poor thing.

Abby suddenly gets a sharp pain in her stomach.

Claudia: *(Panicking)* My God, are you OK?

Abby: Yeah. I just keep getting these pains. They go away though.

Claudia: It's the stress of it all. Having a child is not an easy thing.

Abby: Tell me about it!

Debs: (***Shouting and standing up***) How much longer do I have to bloody wait?

Claudia: Please, can you not shout?

Debs: *(Shouting)* I can shout as loud as I want.

Claudia: The girl isn't feeling very well… please.

Debs looks at Abby. She slowly sits down.

Claudia: Thank you.

They fall silent for a few seconds.

Debs: Bloody men!

Claudia: Very true.

Abby: I hate them.

Claudia giggles.

Claudia: They are very annoying at times.

Debs: My fella, well I call him my fella but we don't live together, he's a bit of a… well… a plonker. We've been together for nearly three months now and he's never stayed over at mine. Sounds dodgy don't it?

Claudia: *(Cautiously)* Honestly? Yes, it does sound a tad mysterious.

Debs: I know. So I asked him. I said "Oi, you little bastard, are you cheating on me?"

Abby: And what did he say?

Debs: He just took my hands, looked me in the eyes and said *(Softly)* "Sweetheart… why would I cheat on the best I've ever had?".

Abby: *(Sarcastically)* Nice!

Claudia: I find that men do have a way with words.

Debs: *(Irate)* You saying he's lying or something?

Claudia: I'm just saying that not all men can be trusted.

Debs: *(Getting louder)* Well I'm sorry Miss Perfect; we can't all have a perfect life with a perfect husband.

Claudia: *(Dismissive)* Perfect? You know nothing.

Silence.

Abby: How long have you been married?

Claudia: Nearly five years now.

Abby: Was your baby planned?

Claudia: *(Confused)* Planned? Not quite, no. But I am so happy. I can't wait to be a mother.

Abby: Does your husband not want the baby?

Claudia: *(Offended)* I beg your pardon?

Abby: *(Softly)* You just seem so… sad. Like you're missing something. Does he not want the baby?

Pause.

Claudia: *(Voice breaking)* I don't know. We don't really see each other very often. He's just so busy at work. He starts early, finishes late. He just doesn't seem interested anymore.

Abby: Where does he work?

Claudia: He works for Atkins and Co. A large pharmaceutical company in the town centre.

Abby looks visible unnerved.

Claudia: I keep saying to him that I need his help but… I get nothing back.

Debs: *(Provokingly)* See… not so perfect after all. Kev would never treat me like that.

Claudia: *(Confused)* Kev? How did you know his name?

Debs: *(Confused)* Who?

Claudia: My husband... Kevin.

Debs: *(Provokingly)* My fella is called Kev. It's a popular name love; it's not just reserved for the poshes and toffs!

Claudia: Are you this nasty all the time? Or are you just having a really bad day?

Debs: *(Shouting)* Ay! Don't you pasteurise me!

Claudia: *(Sarcastically)* I think you mean patronise, sweetheart.

Debs: *(Squaring up to Claudia)* Oh don't think I won't flatten a pregnant bitch.

Claudia: Are you threatening me?

Debs: Yeah... what you gonna do about it?

Claudia gets her phone out and dials.

Claudia: Hello. This is Claudia Perkins-Smith, can you please put me through to my husband Kevin Perkins.

Debs grabs the phone from Claudia

Claudia: *(Outraged)* What the hell do you think you're doing?

Debs: What is your husband's name?

Claudia: Give me back my phone!

Debs: *(Getting louder)* What is your husband's name?

Claudia: You know his name. It's Kevin. Now give me back my phone!

Debs: *(Getting louder)* What's his name, his full name?

Claudia: For goodness sake. His name is Kevin George Perkins. His date of birth is 6th May 1975. His star sign is Taurus. He wears a size nine shoe and his favourite food is Chilli Con Carne! Is that enough information for you?

Debs sinks to her chair. Claudia grabs the phone and holds it to her ear.

Claudia: Brilliant they've gone.

Debs: *(Almost to herself)* Kevin.

Claudia: *(Bluntly)* What is the meaning of this?

Debs: *(Softly)* It's Kevin.

Claudia: What are you blabbering on about Kevin? When my husband hears about this he'll…

Debs: *(Louder)* It's my Kev.

Pause.

Claudia: *(Confused)* Pardon?

Debs: It's my Kev… your Kevin is my Kev.

Claudia laughs.

Claudia: Well you've completely lost the plot now. *(Angrily)* I'm not going to stand here and listen to such drivel.

Claudia goes to leave.

Debs: Here… look at this picture.

She holds out her mobile phone.

Debs: It's last month… at my youngest lad's birthday. He brought him a present… here.

Claudia slowly takes the phone. She sinks to her chair as she looks at it.

Claudia: *(Quietly)* This is a joke. You're playing a game… a sick, sick game…

Debs: I'm not. Your Kevin… is my Kev.

Pause.

Claudia: *(Standing up and shouting)* You dirty whore, how could you? He's married!

Debs: *(Shouting)* I didn't know that, honest.

Claudia: Whatever.

Debs: *(Offended)* Ay! I'm a lot of things but a cheater I am not.

Claudia: Liar! You're a liar. This is a sick, sick twisted joke and I will not listen to this anymore.

Claudia goes to leave again.

Abby: She's not lying.

Claudia stops.

Claudia: *(Confused)* What? What do you mean? How do you know?

Abby: *(Hesitantly)* Your Kevin… her Kev… he's… well… he's my baby's father.

Silence. Eventually Claudia sits back down.

Abby: I work with him, at the company in town. We're not a couple or anything. It was just one time… one night.

Silence.

Claudia: *(Softly)* When?

Silence.

Claudia: *(More direct)* When?

Abby: New Year. There was a company party and I had just split up with my boyfriend so I went alone. I didn't go looking for anything, honest, in fact… I was so drunk I don't really remember…

Claudia: *(Angry)* You mean you got my husband drunk and…

Abby: *(Trying to convince)* No, that's not what happened at all. He was being nice to me and kept buying me drinks. I was feeling so hammered that I told him I didn't want another one but he called me a party pooper and bought me one anyway. Before I knew it he'd bought me four or five more and I could hardly stand up.

Claudia: If you were so drunk how the hell do you know all this?

Abby: A girl I worked with told me. She said that he... Kevin... took me to the bathroom. But we didn't go to the bathroom because I remember being in the office next door. The lights were out... and then... I passed out.

Silence.

Debs: *(Carefully)* Are you saying what I think you're saying? Did he... force himself on you?

Claudia: *(Incensed)* Don't be so stupid, he would never...

Debs: *(Louder)* Did he force himself on you?

Silence.

Abby: *(Quietly)* I don't know. I just remember waking up and... he was getting dressed... and then he left. Now he just keeps calling me, saying he loves me and wants us to be together. Just us two.

Claudia stands.

Claudia: This is ridiculous. I am not going to stay here and listen to these lies.

Debs: **(Bluntly)** Oh wake up you daft cow, this ain't no joke.

Debs sits down.

Debs: *(Softly)* I can't believe my Kev is your Kev and your Kev.

Abby: *(Adamantly)* He isn't my Kev.

Claudia: *(Forceful)* No he's mine and he wouldn't do this to me. He just wouldn't.

Claudia sits down in tears.

Abby: I can't believe this is happening.

Debs: He said he loved me. Bastard.

Long pause.

Abby: What do we do now?

Debs: I don't know.

Abby: Claudia?

Claudia does not answer.

Abby: Should we call him?

Debs: And give him a chance to worm his way out of this? No way.

Abby: *(Pleading)* But we can't let him get away with this. Claudia, what do you think?

Claudia does not answer.

Debs: Maybe we should set a trap, so that we're all there and he has to face us all at the same time.

Abby: Do you think that would work?

Debs: Worth a try, I say.

Claudia: *(Forcing back the tears)* Listen to you. Talking as though this is a game. This is my husband we're talking about. This is my life.

Debs: Well you got any better ideas?

Silence.

Claudia: *(Softly)* I love him.

Silence.

Debs: *(Softly)* So do I.

Silence.

Claudia: How could he do this to me?

Silence.

Claudia: What a bastard.

Debs: *(Louder)* That's better. He is a bastard.

Abby: A total bastard.

Debs: The biggest bastard I've ever known.

Silence.

Claudia: *(Softly)* But I love him.

Silence.

Debs: *(Softly)* So do I.

Abby takes control.

Abby: Come on. This man is a cheat. He's a liar. You can't be in love with a man like this.

Claudia: I need to speak to him.

Claudia starts to call him from her phone.

Debs: No I need to speak to him first.

Debs starts to call him from her mobile.

Abby: *(Pleading)* This is stupid. Look at you both. You're embarrassing yourself. He's a rat, a dirty cheating rat. Put your phones away, don't do this.

Claudia: Why isn't he answering?

Abby: Claudia, please, don't do this. He's not worth it.

Claudia: *(With venom)* I'm not stupid you know. I know what you're doing. You want me to leave him so you can have him for yourself.

Abby: *(Shocked)* What? No, that's not true, he keeps phoning me, I don't want anything to do with him.

Claudia: *(With hatred)* You're the liar. But I've figured you out, you dirty little whore but you won't win. He's my husband, mine.

Debs: Is that true?

Abby: What? No, I don't want him.

Debs: *(Adamantly)* Well you won't get him, he loves me.

Claudia: This is stupid. Kevin just pick up your phone.

Abby gets a pain in her stomach.

Debs: We're not falling for that one. Come on Kev.

Abby: Argh it really hurts.

Claudia: Shh, I can't hear if it's ringing.

Abby: Arghh, please call the nurse.

Debs: Kev is that you? It's Debs. Where are you?

Claudia grabs the phone from Debs.

Claudia: *(Panicking)* Kevin... hello... hello.

Abby: Argh! Please it hurts.

Debs: Oh my God. *(Debs quickly moves to Abby)* Just breathe, come on now, and breathe.

Eventually Abby calms down.

Debs: Better?

Abby: Yeah.

Claudia: Why isn't he answering?

Debs: This is stupid. What are we doing?

Silence.

Claudia: *(Softly)* But he's my husband.

Abby: There's one way to sort this out. Sit here.

The three women sit next to each other. Abby takes a picture of all three of them.

Debs: *(Confused)* What are you doing?

Abby: This man does not deserve either of you. But if you really wanna know who he wants to be with... let me send him this photo. My guess is whoever he loves… he'll call first.

Claudia: *(Pleading)* No… don't.

Abby: Why not.

Claudia: What if he doesn't call me?

Abby: You need to know.

Silence.

Claudia: OK.

Abby sends the message.

Abby: Sent.

Debs: Now what?

Abby: We wait.

All three women hold their mobile phones in their hands. We hear the sound of a phone ringing.

The End